The Maine Play Book

A Four-Season Guide to Family Fun and Adventure

ISLANDPORT PRESS

ISLANDPORT PRESS

Islandport Press
P.O. Box 10
Yarmouth, Maine 04096
www.islandportpress.com
books@islandportpress.com

All photos in *The Maine Play Book*, unless otherwise credited, are by the author or courtesy of Islandport Press. Cover photos (clockwise from top left): Courtesy of Winterberry Farm; Courtesy of Maine Office of Tourism; Courtesy of Songo River Queen; Courtesy of Teresa Lagrange.

ISBN: 978-1-952143-15-1
Library of Congress Control Number: 2017952149

Dean L. Lunt, Publisher
Book design by Teresa Lagrange, Islandport Press

Printed in the USA by Versa Press

To Ted, Lauren, and Will—here's to a lifetime of adventures together.

And tho' we seek far and wide
Our search will be in vain,
To find a fairer spot on earth
Than Maine! Maine! Maine!

—from *State of Maine Song*, Roger Vinton Snow

McLaughlin Garden, South Paris

Contents

Author Jennifer Hazard with her children
Photo by Cathy Davis

Introduction

When Islandport Press first published this book in 2018, my children were 11 and 12 years old. So much has changed in that time. My son and daughter are teenagers now with independent spirits. Our world, and how we navigate our day-to-day as a family, has also changed dramatically.

The first edition of *The Maine Play Book* not only captured the adventures of my young family throughout our state, but provided a glimpse into a time where we could visit the open spaces and events we loved most without worrying about our health or the health of others. Now more than ever, it's always a good idea to plan, call ahead, check websites for updates and be flexible. Throughout the pandemic, everyone has needed to pivot and understand that changes can happen at any time.

It's important to respect the rules that Maine State Parks, land trusts, farms, and other organizations have put into place for public health and safety. Some may require reservations or tickets before you go, and others might limit numbers. If you're visiting an outdoor space, you might also want to consider going at an off-peak time to avoid crowds. Whether your family is planning a day at the beach or on the trail, the outdoors are best enjoyed at quieter times when you can hear the sounds of the natural world around you.

The good news is the spaces in this book can be a path towards relaxation and respite. During this challenging time in history, my family and I have taken full advantage of the beauty of the Maine outdoors. Just as we did when my kids were small, we buoyed our spirits with road trips throughout our home state. Together, we've camped and hiked in some of our favorite state parks, explored ponds and lakes with our canoe, or simply enjoyed a campfire in our own backyard.

The outdoors has remained a source of joy and healing for my family and me, no matter what the world throws our way. I hope the ideas presented in the book will help you find the same.

Sebago Lakes region
Photo by Melissa Kim

How to Use This Book

The Maine Play Book is divided in sections by the seasons. In each chapter, you'll find suggestions for outdoor exploration, pick-your-own farms, and festivals to enjoy by regions of the state, including **Southern Points**, **Midcoast**, **Lakes & Mountains,** and **Downeast & Northern Points**.

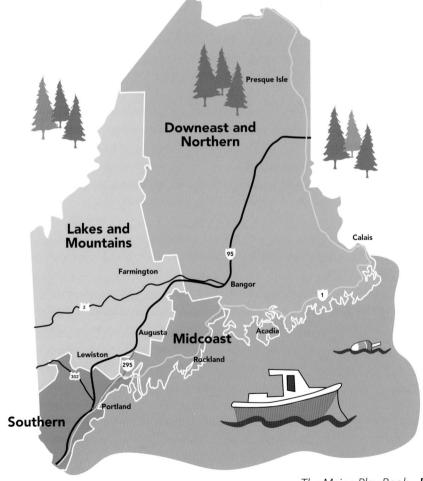

Presque Isle

Downeast and Northern

Lakes and Mountains

Calais

Farmington

95

Bangor

2

1

Augusta **Midcoast** Acadia

Lewiston Rockland

302 295

Southern Portland

Southern

Beloved for its expansive
beaches, cool little cities,
and walkable towns.

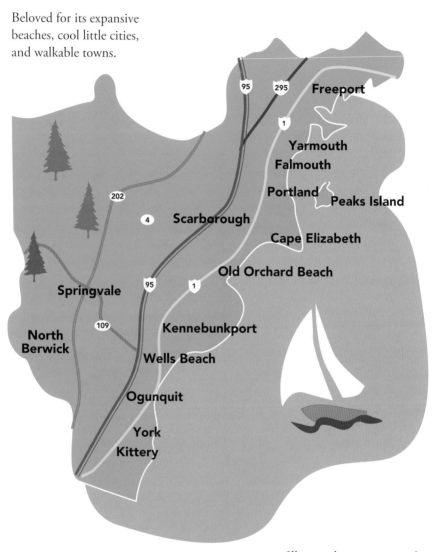

95 295 **Freeport**

1

Yarmouth
Falmouth

Portland

202 **Peaks Island**

4 **Scarborough**

Cape Elizabeth

Old Orchard Beach

95 1

Springvale

109 **Kennebunkport**

North
Berwick

Wells Beach

Ogunquit

York
Kittery

Illustrated maps not to scale

Midcoast

Scenic coastal villages and
magical natural spaces make
the Midcoast a joy to visit.

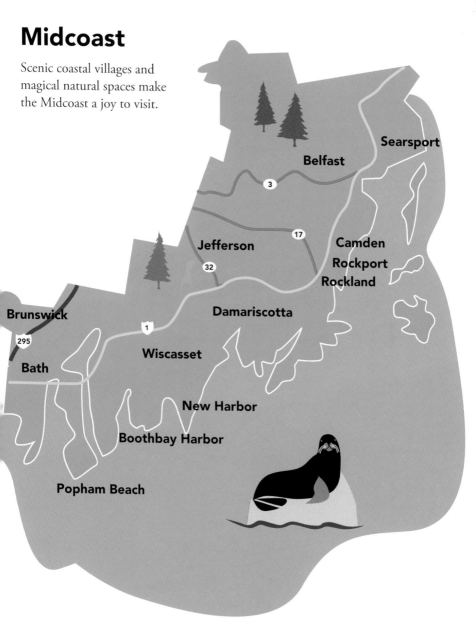

Searsport

Belfast

3

17

Jefferson

32

Camden
Rockport
Rockland

Brunswick

295

1

Damariscotta

Wiscasset

Bath

New Harbor

Boothbay Harbor

Popham Beach

Lakes and Mountains

For hiking, freshwater swimming, or skiing, this part of the state is worth exploring.

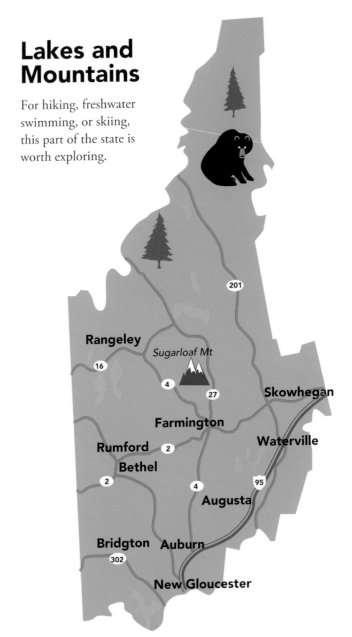

Rangeley

Sugarloaf Mt

16

4

27

Skowhegan

Farmington

Rumford

2

Waterville

Bethel

2

4

95

Augusta

Bridgton

Auburn

302

New Gloucester

201

Downeast and Northern

This part of the state is a well-kept secret with its rugged beauty and dramatic spaces.

Presque Isle

Allagash Waterway

Baxter State Park

1

95

Millinocket

Greenville

Dover-Foxcroft

9

Eastport

Bangor

1

Ellsworth

Bar Harbor
Southwest Harbor

As a parent, I understand that your adventures need to be tailored to suit the ages of your children, so you'll find suggestions for age-appropriate experiences. I've also tried to keep the majority of suggestions budget-friendly, but whenever there are significant fees involved I've noted them.

You'll find three icons that appear with some of the entries. The binoculars icon 🔭 indicates nearby places where you might find something more to see or do. The fork and knife icon 🍴 tells you where you might find family-friendly dining options nearby, which can range from casual roadside cafes to ice cream shops and restaurants. The accessible icon ♿ marks outdoor spaces and adventures that are wheelchair-friendly. Note that several state parks and beaches have some accessible trails. To learn more visit **Maine's Accessible Outdoors** at parksandlands.com.

If you're in search of organizations that foster inclusive communities outdoors, other great resources include **Outdoor Afro** (outdoorafro.com), **Teens to Trails** (teenstotrails.org), and **The Venture Out Project** (ventureoutproject.com).

If you're looking for ideas for road trips, the back of the book gives you a few itineraries by region and season (page 170). Remember that these are purely suggestions, and many of the places I've called attention to are ideal to visit any time of year. Similarly, you'll find a comprehensive, at-a-glance list of all of the outdoor spaces mentioned (page 164).

Outdoor exploration in fields and forests makes for a fun family outing most anytime of year, but there's no denying the allure of Maine's lakes and ocean beaches. Some of my family's favorite places to swim are shared in the summer section, but if you want to see them all in a quick list of fresh and saltwater swimming, check page 162.

On those days when the weather requires indoor play, children's museums are always a good option. Little ones will especially enjoy the creative play spaces, interactive exhibits, and opportunities for dress up. You'll find four to choose from throughout the state, including the **Children's Museum and Theatre of Maine** (www.kitetails.org) in Portland, **Coastal Children's Museum** (coastalchildrensmuseum.org) in Rockland, **Children's Discovery Museum** (childrensdiscoverymuseum.org) in Augusta, and **Maine Discovery Museum** (www.mainediscoverymuseum.org) in Bangor. Before you go check the web sites for admission fees, hours, and special events.

Pick-your-own farms and seasonal festivals are also great locations for families to spend a day together. Kids learn about where the food comes from, visit with animals, participate in quirky contests, and so much more. You'll discover some of the tried-and-true farms and festivals I've come to enjoy year after year throughout each section. If you're wondering when the best time of year is to pick blueberries or peaches, the back of the book details a full list of What to Pick When (see page 161). You'll also find a handy, monthly list of festivals throughout the state (see page 158). Be sure to check it often so you don't miss your favorite event.

No matter what adventure you choose, I hope you and your family will fall in love with the beautiful state that I'm so proud to call home.

Preparing for Your Adventure

For families who are planning an adventure outdoors, consider the weather and season. Whether you're venturing outside in the spring, summer, or fall, bottled water, a simple first-aid kit, sunscreen, a quick change of clothes, and bug spray are good to have on hand. These days, with Lyme Disease on the rise, it's important to check your family for ticks after spending time on the trails (simple tick removers are available at most pharmacies).

Since the weather is fickle here in Maine, packing warm layers is a smart idea no matter the season. Keeping an extra sweatshirt or fleece in the car comes in handy and during the winter months even more so. Extra socks, hats, mittens, and even a change of boots are welcome after a day out in the snow. And with the sun reflecting up from the snow, sunscreen is necessary to bring along in the winter, too.

If you're heading outdoors from October through December, it's also important to wear blaze orange (you can find hats, scarves, and other gear at hardware stores and sporting outfitters like L.L.Bean). Most state parks and preserves will post signs during hunting season at the entrance. However, be sure to call ahead or check park websites for hunting statuses before you go.

With a little preparation and good sense, you're sure to have an adventure to remember!

Spring

Spring weather in Maine is tricky. March and April can feel like a long extension of winter. Snow cover can still blanket the ground, which later transforms to a muddy landscape. This is the time of year when the weather might require indoor play (see page 10 for options). By May, we catch glimpses of the good things to come—the trees begin to bud, the crocuses sprout up from the brown earth, and on the sunniest of days, it's not unusual to see runners, bikers, dog walkers, and parents pushing jogging strollers soaking up the warmer weather. Beautiful spring days like these are meant to savor.

Spring Walks + Biking

During this time of year, when the ground conditions vary, it's important to be smart about where you walk or bike and how you plan. My family often seeks out parks or spaces with paved or well-traversed trails. Dirt trails can be muddy in March and April, so bringing along Wellies or rubber boots for walks is always a good idea.

Southern

Smith Preserve
76 Guinea Road
Kennebunkport
(207) 967-3465
kporttrust.org

This stunning preserve has more than 10 miles of well-marked trails for families and their pets. In late spring there's nothing better than walking over bridges, listening to the sound of snow melt running through brooks and experiencing the forest coming back to life. The 1.7-mile Brook Loop is a hilly walk that takes you near waterfalls. For a unique experience, access the 4.8-mile Trolley Loop via the **Seashore Trolley Museum** (trolleymuseum.org), the largest electric railway museum in the world. Beginning in May, guests of the museum can get a trolley ride to the trails, depart the trolley and explore the preserve. Trolleys depart every 45 minutes. Mountain bikes are welcome at the preserve and on the trolley.

Bug Light Park + Greenbelt Walkway
Madison Street (off Broadway)
South Portland
(207) 767-7650
southportland.org

On the first warm spring day of the season, our family loves to visit this urban park, which is home to the 19th-century Portland Breakwater "Bug" Light—a charming lighthouse known for its diminutive size and Greek-inspired design. The 6+-acre park has plenty of open space, and dogs are welcome. For bikers, it's also the trailhead to the 5.6-mile one-way Greenbelt Walkway, a paved trail which meanders through Mill Creek Park, residential neighborhoods, woods, and open fields. Arrows on the road will keep you moving in the right direction. If you have little ones, be prepared to cross four busy intersections—three at Mill Creek and the other on Broadway and Evans Street. The trail ends at Wainwright Recreation Complex parking lot.

Bug Light Park, South Portland

Scratch Baking Co. (scratchbakingco. com) is a beloved little bakeshop in South Portland where you'll find homemade pastries, coffee, and more good things to eat. We like to bring their famous chewy bagels to Bug Light Park to fuel up before a bike ride.

Mackworth Island

Andrews Avenue (off US Route 1)
Falmouth
(207) 688-4712
maine.gov/mackworthisland

This is a popular place among locals for its easy access to shoreline and forest. Little ones also love the fairy house village located along the pathway. Dogs on leashes are welcome here and the wide, 1.25-mile-loop trail makes for easy exploration. My kids like to walk down to the beach (you'll find steps along the way to take you there) and explore the rocks along the shore.

Royal River Park

103 East Elm Street (across from Yarmouth Historical Society)
Yarmouth
(207) 846-2406
yarmouthcommunityservices.org

This community park is where my children spent their preschool years and where we walked our greyhound on a daily basis. You'll find a looping path, totaling 2.6 miles, that winds through the park along the Royal River and past the remnants of an historic mill. Kids will love viewing the falls and rushing water (there's a lookout point early in the walk). You will also discover spots along the way to reach the river, and it's not unusual to see black herons standing on river stones in search of fish.

There are several options for easy walks—the main trail leads to a three-way connector, which provides options to walk into town or along US Route 1's Beth Congdon Pathway. Turn right and walk up towards the elementary school, where you'll find a playground for little ones. While you may have to stop and start for dogs and pedestrians, the park is also a fun place to bike.

Mast Landing Audubon Sanctuary

65 Upper Mast Landing Road
Freeport
(207) 781-2330
maineaudubon.org

If you are looking for a quiet escape from Freeport's outlet center, this 101-acre Audubon Sanctuary is your answer. There are five short forest trails to choose from, each with its own unique offerings. The 1.6-mile round-trip Ridge

Trail takes you to an old dam site and historic mill-master's house, which is currently home to Mast Landing's caretakers. In the springtime, you may spot wild trillium flowers along the trail and shorebirds in the tidal marsh. It's an ideal place to explore with young hikers.

Midcoast

Androscoggin River Bicycle Path
Water Street (past Water Street Boat Landing 2)
Brunswick
(207) 725-6656
brunswickme.org

This two-way bike path, which is 2.6 miles each way, is known for its wide, paved lane that runs along the Andro-scoggin River. It can also be accessed in Cook's Corner, Brunswick (Grover Lane) and in Topsham (Elm Street). Parents will appreciate the flat pathway and quick access to clean outhouses. If your kids need a break, there are picnic spots along the way. **Note:** Leashed dogs, walkers and runners are all welcome on the trail, so be prepared to navigate around them on weekends.

Cathance River Preserve
Highland Green Village (off Route 196)
Topsham
(207) 331-3202
creamaine.org

With more than 5 miles of trails to choose from, this 235-acre preserve gives families the opportunity to walk through peaceful woods, explore a vast heath, or hear the rush and roar of the Cathance River from the Rapids Connector trail. Mid-May is an ideal time to visit as there are few bugs and trillium are in bloom. The preserve is also home to an Ecology Center (open Sundays noon to 2 p.m.) that's housed in a recycled post and beam barn. **Note:** You'll drive through the privately owned Highland Green Village—a 55+ community—before reaching the Ecology Center parking lot.

Merryspring Nature Center
30 Conway Road (off US Route 1)
Camden
(207) 236-2239
merryspring.org

My family attended a friend's wedding at this 66-acre park, and since then, it's remained a favorite for its meandering trails, gardens, and tucked-away places to sit and take in its quiet beauty. There

Maine Wildlife Park, Gray
Photo by Tamra Wight

are several easy trails to choose for exploring. If you're a first-time visitor, the 1-mile loop Perimeter Trail is a good way to get to know the park. Merryspring is also known for its family programming, so be sure to check their online calendar for events before you go.

Ocean Point Walk
Shore Road (off Route 96)
East Boothbay

This relaxed walk, which is located on a residential peninsula in East Boothbay, is ideal for families of all ages. On a narrow, 2-mile stretch of road, kids can walk the rocks along the ocean's edge or explore Grimes Cove at low tide. Dogs are welcome and there is plenty of available parking on Grimes Avenue before you reach Shore Road.

 If it's a beautiful spring day, pick up picnic sandwiches at **East Boothbay General Store** (ebgs.us), which is conveniently located on Route 96.

Belfast Rail Trail
City Point Road
Belfast
(207) 338-3370 x127
coastalmountains.org

Known as "The Passy," this crushed-stone trail was once was the corridor for the Belfast & Moosehead Lake Railroad, a passenger and freight line that operated from 1871 to 2007. Today the 2.3-mile, one-way trail is wheelchair accessible and open to pedestrians and cyclists. The tree-lined trail begins in downtown Belfast at the Armistice Footbridge (Footbridge Road) and continues along the Passagassawakeag River to the City Point Central Railroad Museum (13 Oak Hill Road), where you'll find historic railroad cars, cabooses, and a steam engine.

Lakes and Mountains

Maine Wildlife Park
56 Game Farm Road (Route 26A)
Gray
(207) 657-4977
maine.gov/ifw/wildlife-park

For little ones, the wildlife park is perfect for a morning or afternoon of exploration. Many of the animals who live here were rescued and could not fend for themselves in the wild. Kids will delight in seeing some of their favorite animals up close, including black bears, mountain lions, eagles, and even moose. The park is also home to gardens, tree-lined trails, and a fish hatchery. There's a picnic area, a snack shack for sweet treats, and a nature

store. There is a modest admission fee.
Note: Maine Wildlife Park opens in mid-April and closes in November.

Sebago to the Sea Trail: Otter Ponds to Route 202
Johnson Field Access Point
89 Chadbourne Road
Standish
sebagotothesea.org

Suitable for children ages 8 and up, this 6-mile section (one-way) through Standish, Gorham, and Windham combines unpaved and paved sections of the Mountain Division Trail and the Sebago to the Sea Trail, and is best for mountain biking. With the exception of one steep hill at Otter Pond in Standish, it's a fairly easy ride. Your family will need to cross over a few roads along the way, and while most are quiet, you'll want to pay close attention at main crossings. There are benches for breaks along the trail. If you have little ones or a stroller, use the Shaw Park entrance (55 Partridge Lane, Gorham) of the Sebago to the Sea Trail, where you'll find convenient parking. Walkers and bikers will enjoy the mile-long paved Gambo Dam Loop.

Kennebec River Rail Trail
MSHA Parking Lot
Water Street
Augusta
krrt.org

This scenic 6.5-mile paved trail follows the defunct Augusta-Portland rail line and is a part of the developing East Coast Greenway, which runs from Florida to Maine. This one-way section, which connects the towns of Augusta, Hallowell, Farmingdale, and Gardiner, is a popular spot for bikers, runners, and dog walkers (it's also wheelchair accessible). There's much to see on the trail— bustling downtowns, waterfalls, rushing brooks, and osprey flying overhead.

Bethel Pathway
Davis Park Picnic Area, Route 26
Bethel
(207) 200-8240
mainetrailfinder.com

Cyclists and walkers alike enjoy this 3.4-mile roundtrip pathway that starts in the heart of the village. At Davis Park, you'll find a covered bridge, a playground, a skate park, and picnic tables. Continue on the path and you'll find an impressive bridge over the Androscoggin River.

Orono Bog Walk, Bangor

Along the way, you'll spot Old Speck, Puzzle, and Baldpate mountains. The one-way trail is handicapped-accessible and is made of pavement and crushed stone; there are benches along the trail should you need a quick break. Dogs on leash are welcome on the trail, but not in the park.

Downeast and Northern

Orono Bog Boardwalk
Tripp Drive
Bangor
(207) 866-2578
umaine.edu/oronobogwalk

This scenic, 1-mile loop walk is a treat for young families, especially because the trail is entirely made up of planked boardwalk. At the trailhead, you'll find a picnic table and shelter, should you want to bring breakfast or lunch. Begin by walking through a dense green wetland that opens up to a vast bog, which is home to a variety of birds, plants, and wildflowers. The boardwalk is stroller- and wheelchair-friendly, and you'll find several benches for respite along the way. **Note:** The boardwalk opens in early May.

If you have older children and are searching for more trails to cover, the Orono Bog is part of the 650-acre **Bangor City Forest** (cityforest.bangorinfo. com), where you'll find 10 miles of hiking and cycling trails.

Bar Harbor Shore Path
Ells Pier (trailhead)
Bar Harbor
barharborvia.gov

This gravel path is popular among tourists and locals for good reason. In the springtime, before the tourist season is in full swing, visitors can enjoy a peaceful walk along the Bar Harbor waterfront. You'll pass the stately Bar Harbor Inn and historic mansions. Kids can climb down on the rocks, build small cairns, and look out toward the Porcupine Islands and the Schoodic Peninsula. Balance Rock, a giant boulder left along the shoreline from the last ice age, is also a highlight. The walk is only 0.75 miles

one-way, but it's an excellent introduction to the town of Bar Harbor.

Wonderland Trail
Seawall Road/102A
Southwest Harbor
(207) 288-3338
mainetrailfinder.com

This relaxed walk, which is only 1.4 miles round-trip through a forest trail dotted with spruce and fir trees, brings you to the edge of Bennett Cove, complete with rocky ledges and tall pines. Young children can explore tidepools at low tide, or dip their feet in the water on a warm spring day. Parking is available at the trailhead.

👀 Located less than 1.5 miles away, the iconic **Bass Harbor Head Light** in Tremont (nps.gov/acad) is worth a visit. The lighthouse, which was built in 1858 on a cliff, stands 56 feet above the water. Kids can climb the rocks to get a closer look.

Nordic Heritage Center
Off Fort Fairfield Road (Route 167)
Presque Isle
nordicheritagecenter.org

In Northern Maine, spring skiing can last well into April, but once the snow melts and the trails are clear, mountain

Bass Harbor Head Light, Tremont

biking at the Nordic Heritage Center (see page 125) in May is a treat. The 20-plus miles of forested biking trails were created by Rich Edwards, a trail design expert from the International Mountain Biking Association. Depending on your family's skill level, you can choose from smooth, flat beginner trails to more challenging, technical trails. The trails are open to walkers and runners, plus there is a designated trail at the entrance for dog walkers.

Wonderland Trail, Southwest Harbor

Farm Visits

Springtime in Maine officially kicks off with **Maine Maple Sunday**—a statewide celebration of the sap running from the maple trees after a long winter. Traditionally, the celebrations take place on the fourth Sunday in March, but more farms are hosting events throughout the weekend.

Spring is also a time when farms are brimming with newborn animals. My family loves to visit local farms to meet the baby goats, lambs, and chicks.

Southern

Horse Island Camp
Island Breeze Farm
Peaks Island, Portland
(207) 838-7652
horseislandcamp.com

Take the Peaks Island Ferry (see page 44) for an unforgettable experience at Horse Island Camp. Owner Jeanie Alves, who has been teaching horseback riding for nearly 20 years, offers guided tours that are tailored to any riding ability. You'll ride down island dirt roads and hiking paths along the scenic shoreline. Riders can choose from a 60- or 90-minute-excursions and rides are designed for ages 3 and up. **Note:** Horse Island Camp is a 15-20 minute walk from the ferry. Jeanie provides detailed directions; however, if you prefer not to walk, the Peaks Island Taxi (207-518-0000) will meet you at the ferry. Just be sure to call in advance of your arrival, and bring a car seat for small children.

Merrifield Farm
195 North Gorham Road
Gorham
(207) 892-5061

This popular sugaring farm celebrates all things maple on the fourth Saturday and Sunday of March. There is so much to see, including a rustic sugarhouse, a 1900s ice house and barn, and a playground for little ones. During your visit, check out the blacksmithing and ox demonstrations plus a display of antiques used for maple sugaring. The farm offers a pancake breakfast, but there are also smoked cheeses, maple roasted nuts, and maple creemees (soft serve ice cream) on hand.

If you're unable to get to Merrifield

Farm on **Maine Maple Sunday**, but still want to try their delicious products, simply call in advance of your visit.

Smiling Hill Farm

781 County Road (Route 22)
Westbrook
(207) 775-4818
smilinghill.com

This historic family farm (see page 120) is popular with locals and travelers for its year-round dairy store, which includes flavored milks in glass bottles, ice cream, artisanal cheeses, and yogurts. At the end of April, the farm's barnyard opens for the season. For a small fee, children can visit with the farm animals and play on the large wooden structures, which include a truck, an airplane, and train. There are two petting areas where kids can meet the sheep and goats. The farm also plays host to several events throughout the spring, including an Easter egg hunt and baby goat snuggling sessions.

Sunflower Farm Creamery
12 Harmon Way
Cumberland
(207) 829-8347
sunflowerfarm.info

Sunflower Farm has become well-known over the years for a viral video that documents their baby goats going for an energetic morning run. Mid-April through June, the farm opens its doors to visitors for baby goat snuggling sessions. The Nigerian dwarf kids have bright eyes, soft fur, and perky ears, making them irresistible to children and adults alike. It's impossible not to smile while holding them. If you visit in mid-May, the self-serve shop opens on Saturdays for good things like chevre, goat milk caramels, and creamy goat milk fudge.

Midcoast

Northern Solstice Alpaca Farm
141 Crosby Brook Road
Unity
(207) 356-4146
mainealpacaexperience.com

It's clear how much the alpacas are loved at this impeccable farm, which is located directly across the street from the Common Ground Fairgrounds (see page 110).

Owners Robin and Corry Pratt radiate enthusiasm about their animals and just how much fun they are to raise. Their free farm tours, which take place Tuesday through Sunday, teach families all about these curious creatures. You'll even get to meet the animals face to face. The month of May is a great time to visit. The farm hosts a shearing day, where visitors can watch the shearing process. The farm also has a cozy gift shop, where guests can find cozy socks, colorful scarves, and more unique offerings.

Sable Oak Equestrian Center
38 Bridge Road
Brunswick
(207) 443-4006
sableoakec.com

This skilled horseback riding center offers classes for all levels of riders throughout the year. Owner Sherrye Trafton provides half-hour to full-hour lessons at the farm. Visitors can also try guided Adventure Rides on Trafton's seasoned school horses. You can ride at **Popham Beach** in Phippsburg (see page 55). The beach rides, which run from October to March 31, cost more but are worth the unique experience. Be sure to call in advance to book your ride.

Copper Tail Farm
293 Genthner Road
Waldoboro
(541) 729- 5769
coppertailfarm.com

This small family farm raises dairy goats and makes everything from goat milk soap, cheeses, and yogurt to creamy goat milk caramels and cajeta—a delicious caramel sauce for ice cream or fruit slices. In April, the farm teams up with two other area farms for a **Kid Hugging Day**, where visitors can snuggle with the goats and stock up on local cheeses. Beginning in May, the farm is open to visitors on Sundays from 8 a.m. to 6 p.m.

 Copper Tail Farm is a part of the **Midcoast Cheese Trail** which includes Pumpkin Vine Family Farm (pumpkinvinefamilyfarm.com), Fuzzy Udder Creamery (fuzzyudder.com), East Forty Farm (lakinsgorgescheese.com), and Toddy Pond Farm (toddypond-farm.com). All of the farms are open to visitors and host special events throughout the year.

Copper Tail Farm, Waldoboro
Photo by Jenny Nelson, Wylde Photography

The Morris Farm

156 Gardiner Road (Route 27)
Wiscasset
(207) 882-4080
morrisfarm.org

Morris Farm is a community-based education center, where guests are welcome to tour the barn and grounds. The farm also hosts vacation camps and an annual fair that features local farmers, cheesemakers, and live music. Morris Farm is also home to a small shop that offers locally made honey, maple syrup, milk, eggs, and seasonal veggies.

 If you want to explore more during your visit, the farm connects to the **Wiscasset Community Trail** system, a 200-acre parcel that combines farm trails, the Sortwell Memorial Forest (mainetrailfinder.com), and the town forest. Be sure to wear good boots, as the trails can be muddy in the springtime.

Goranson Farm

250 River Road (Route 128)
Dresden
(207) 737-8834
goransonfarm.me

Rob Johanson, who co-operates Goranson Farm with his wife Jan, has made maple syrup for over 40 years. He's a terrific resource for learning everything families need to know about syrup production. On **Maine Maple Sunday** (the fourth Sunday in March), the certified organic farm also offers hot drinks and horse-drawn rides if there is snow on the ground. During your visit, try their organic maple syrup, free maple sundaes, or locally made maple donuts. If that's not enough to entice you, you can sit and enjoy live music in their spacious greenhouse.

Goranson Farm sells their products at several farmers' markets throughout the year. Through the end of April, you can find them at the Bath, Brunswick, and Portland winter markets (see getrealmaine.com farmers' market directory for details).

Lakes and Mountains

Jillson's Farm and Sugarhouse

143 Jordan Bridge Road
Sabattus
(207) 375-3380
jillsonfarm.com

This is the farm where I first celebrated **Maine Maple Sunday**, and it's where my family and I have returned for many years. Best of all, families aren't limited to just one Sunday in March to visit— you can enjoy their hearty breakfasts every weekend from March through Mother's Day in May. Feast on fluffy pancakes, French toast, eggs, homemade breads, savory baked beans, sausage, and potatoes. If you aren't too full to move after breakfast, meet the animals in the barn or take a tour of the sugarhouse to learn how maple syrup is made.

Nezinscot Farm
284 Turner Center Road
Turner
(207) 225-3231
nezinscotfarm.com

This diversified family farm is best known as the first certified organic dairy in the state and for their beloved yarn and fiber studio. Nezinscot is also home to a sweet cafe that is open for breakfast and lunch on Thursdays through Sundays, where families will find plenty of comfort foods—from light and airy crepes with tempting fillings for breakfast to hearty sandwiches on homemade breads. The farm also hosts two family-friendly events in the springtime, including a **Maine Maple Sunday** brunch in March and a Mother's Day weekend tea in May.

Dunham Farm/Velvet Hollow Sugar Works
29 Dunham Road
Greenwood
(207) 665-2967

Brian and Suzanne Dunham have created a warm and inviting space at Dunham Farm, where guests can enjoy stunning views of the Western Foothills. Brian, who tapped the trees in Velvet Hollow as a young boy, runs the sugarhouse while Suzanne creates gluten-free baked goods in her commercial kitchen. The farm is open all weekend during **Maine Maple Sunday** and offers a special, gluten-free pancake breakfast inside the sugarhouse. Later in the day, guests can enjoy homemade maple turkey chili and thick slices of cornbread for lunch.

If you aren't able to make it to the farm during Maine Maple Sunday, you can find the Dunham's maple syrup, gluten-free baked goods and homemade granola at the Greenwood Farmers' Market (Greenwood Town Hall, Route 26, Locke Mills). The market is open year-round on Fridays from 4 to 6 p.m.

Weston's Farm

48 River Street
Fryeburg
(207) 935-2567
westonsfarm.com

This 18th-century farm in the stunning Saco River Valley is beloved year-round, but in the springtime, hundreds flock to the farm for **Maine Maple Sunday** (the fourth Sunday of March). The Weston family has been making maple syrup for over 150 years. Visit the modest sugarhouse to learn how syrup is made or try a free sample—or two—of maple syrup on ice cream. When the weather gets warmer, Weston's market is also an excellent spot to find seedlings for your garden.

Downeast and Northern

Wild Ivy Farm

2023 Essex Street
Bangor
(207) 942-9658
wildivyfarm.com

Learn to ride from owner Cassie Astle, who has been teaching horseback riding for more than two decades. Her 30-acre training farm offers reasonably priced private lessons and lessons for small groups (up to six) for two hours in the horse arena. For regular students who have more experience, trail rides are also an option. Lessons are for kids ages 5 and up.

Spring Break Maple & Honey

3315 US Route 2
Smyrna
(207) 757-7373
mainemapleandhoney.com

A visit to Spring Break is certain to satisfy any sweet tooth. Partners Kevin and Kristi Brannen produce artisan maple syrup, honey, maple candy, and more delicious treats at their impressive sugarhouse and candy-making facility. You can visit the gift shop or tour the grounds Monday through Saturday. During **Maine Maple Sunday**, families flock to Spring Break throughout the weekend for tours and made-to-order ice cream sundaes with maple syrup.

Spring Events

By the time spring rolls around in Maine, everyone is itching to get outside and enjoy the warmer temperatures. **Maine Maple Sunday** (the fourth weekend in March) kicks off the season with visits to sugar houses and sweet tastings all around the state. When the ground softens, the streams flow, and the lakes begin to thaw, everyone knows that good weather is right around the corner. Come April and May, celebrations pop up in small communities and larger cities as if collectively announcing, "Spring is here!"

Southern

St. Patrick's Day Parade
Commercial Street
Portland
irishofmaine.org

You have to be made of hearty stock to enjoy this parade. In March, the weather is typically windy and cold, but the festive atmosphere makes the parade worth the experience. Hundreds of spectators line Commercial Street wearing their St. Patty's Day finest, and the parade itself features bagpipers, flags from Ireland's 32 counties and Celtic dancers. Slugger the Sea Dog, the Portland Sea Dogs mascot, regularly makes an appearance, too.

🍽 To keep up the festive spirit, we join friends for brunch at Rí Rá (rira.com/portland) after the parade. Located on Commercial Street, the two-story Irish pub offers traditional Irish fare as well as favorites such as French toast with fresh berries and hearty egg sandwiches with smoked bacon. If you're able, get a seat by the window for views of Portland Harbor.

Huttopia Southern Maine Opening Day
149 Sand Pond Road
Sanford
(207) 324-1752
canada-usa.huttopia.com

In May, this unique, tucked away camping spot opens for the season. You can choose to stay in a cozy canvas Trappeur tent, outfitted with a wooden porch, working kitchen, bathroom and soft beds with fresh linens, or opt for an ultra-modern and equally well-appointed tiny house. My family tented waterside, rented paddleboards and canoes to explore the lake, and enjoyed fruit smoothies at the cafe. The campground also has a heated pool, playground and hosts fun events during late spring and summer.

Portland Sea Dogs Opening Day
Hadlock Field, 271 Park Avenue
Portland
(800) 936-3647
seadogs.com

A visit to Portland requires at least one local baseball experience. Sea Dogs games are just right for families of all ages. Of course, there is AA baseball to watch, but my family also likes the kid-friendly contests between innings—including a lively competition of musical chairs on oversized, inflatable seats—and the entertaining antics of the Sea Dogs' mascot, Slugger. And when the Sea Dogs hit a homerun, a little lighthouse rises from the stadium and sounds its foghorn.

Bug Light Kite Festival
Bug Light Park
South Portland
(207) 767-7299
sphistory.org

Watch big, colorful kites take to the skies over Portland Harbor during this festive event, presented by the South Portland Historical Society. Experts from the Nor'easters Kite Club and Kites Over New England teach kite-flying workshops and lead demonstrations on kite-flying. The Bug Light museum gift shop also sells kites and offers food and drink throughout the day. A visit to the event is also an excellent chance to see inside **Bug Light** (see page 14), a 19th-century lighthouse modeled after a Greek monument. Admission is free and parking is available at Southern Maine Community College (Two Fort Road, South Portland).

After the festival, visit **Spring Point Ledge Lighthouse** and Old Fort Preble– a 19th-century military fort. Both are conveniently located on the Southern Maine Community College campus. Families can take a leisurely walk from the fort to a 900-foot breakwater that leads to the lighthouse.

Skyline Farm Plow Day
95 The Lane
North Yarmouth
(207) 829-9203
skylinefarm.org

Visit this historic, working farm to enjoy horse-drawn wagon rides and see powerful draft horses plow the field in preparation for spring plantings. Kids can experience blacksmithing by watching a local expert. Skyline Farm is also home to nearly 2

Portland Sea Dogs, Portland

Skyline Farm Plow Day, North Yarmouth
Photo of J. Luther Gray by Leah Mahoney, courtesy of Skyline Farm

miles of public trails and a historic carriage museum. The event is free to the public and lunch is available for sale.

Midcoast

Copper Tail Farm Kid Hugging Day
293 Genther Road
Waldoboro
(541) 729-5769
coppertailfarm.com

Spring is the best time to visit with baby goats. Copper Tail Farm (page 28) celebrates their arrival with a full day of kid hugging. After a few photo ops and snuggles with the babies and their mamas, your family can shop for fresh chevre and other goat milk products from the farm or visit with local food purveyors and artisans. If you want to meet more baby goats, stop by **Fuzzy Udder Creamery** (fuzzyudder.com), who also open their doors to guests for the day.

Coastal Maine Botanical Gardens Opening Day (♿)
132 Botanical Gardens Drive
Boothbay
(207) 633-8000
mainegardens.org

When the tulips begin to bloom at Coastal Maine Botanical Gardens, the rich colors are nothing short of magical. Visit to view the flowers and enjoy tea and homemade treats in the sunny Kitchen Garden Cafe.

Aldemere Farm Calf Unveiling Day
20 Russell Avenue
Rockport
(207) 236-2739
aldermere.org

This historic saltwater farm and education center hosts a popular annual open house for visitors of all ages. Award-winning Belted Galloways, known for their distinctive black and white stripes, are the stars of the event along with their adorable new baby Belties. During your visit, meet with local cheesemakers and farmers who raise everything from bunnies to goats. You'll also discover tempting local fare, including wood-fired pizza, baked goods, and ice cream. Free admission.

Alewife Festival
Throughout Damariscotta Mills
damariscottamills.org

This wholly unique festival, which celebrates the spawning of thousands of alewives up the Damariscotta River to Damariscotta Lake, is not to be missed.

It's fascinating to see schools of silvery fish travel up (!) a man-made ladder of waterfalls. My children also loved a neighborhood lemonade stand, a creative osprey fishing game, face-painting at Alewives Fabrics, and live bluegrass music. The adults in our group enjoyed fresh local oysters and draughts from nearby Oxbow Brewing Company. Free admission.

Lakes and Mountains

Moose Dash
Rangeley Lakes Trails Center
524 Saddleback Mountain Road
Rangeley
(207) 864-4309
rangeleylakestrailscenter.com

It's true—early March in Maine means there is likely still snow on the ground. The Moose Dash makes the most of the conditions with a lively snowshoe race at the Rangeley Lakes Trails Center. For a modest fee, kids 10 and under can participate in a 1-mile fun run, and older kids up to age 19 can take part in a Junior 5K race. The Moose Dash is also a lot of fun for spectators to watch as it starts and ends in a stadium.

Young at Art
Harlow Gallery
100 Water Street
Hallowell
(207) 622-3813
harlowgallery.org

It's a joy to show kids the work of their peers. This March event, which takes place during Youth Art Month—a nationwide celebration that promotes art and education—highlights the work of local elementary and middle school students. Simultaneously, the adjoining gallery offers a show that complements the students' work. **Note:** Gallery is open Fridays and Saturdays.

Maine Fiddlehead Festival
University of Maine Campus
Farmington
mainefiddleheadfestival.com

This all-ages festival marks the return of the fiddlehead—the fronds of a young fern that are enjoyed as a vegetable. And while little ones might not be enthused by an unusual green veggie, they will enjoy the live music, baby farm animals, games, and crafts. Older kids and adults appreciate the farmers' market, where local produce and crafts are available for purchase. Watch cooking demonstrations and enjoy a locally sourced lunch. Free admission.

McLaughlin Garden Lilac Festival
97 Main Street
South Paris
(207) 743-8820
mclaughlingarden.org

When flowers begin to bloom in Maine after a long winter, it's cause for celebration. I love McLaughlin Garden when the lilacs blossom and their sweet scent carries in the breeze. Kids enjoy exploring among the rows of lilacs while a local musician plays violin. There's also a short trail and a frog pond. For parents, the barn gift shop is full of beautiful objects—from locally made jewelry to colorful pottery. Plants are also for sale during the festival, so you can take home a lilac of your own! Admission is reasonably priced for families.

Downeast and Northern

Can-Am Crown International Sled Dog Races
Main Street
Fort Kent
can-am-crown.net

If you have older children, and don't mind braving the colder temperatures, it is worth traveling to Northern Maine to experience the most challenging sled dog race in the eastern United States. The event—which qualifies teams for the Iditarod—is so much fun for spectators. The 30-, 100-, and 250-mile races all begin on Main Street and end at the Lonesome Pine Trails ski lodge (see page 140).

Eden Farmers Market
Mount Desert Island YMCA
21 Park Street
Bar Harbor
mdifarmersmarkets.com

There's no better way to kick off a spring Sunday than a visit to the farmers market, where your family can get to know local farmers and makers. You'll find maple syrup, fresh bagels and breads, homemade pies, smoked meats, and cheeses alongside seasonal fruits and vegetables. The market runs early May-October from 9 a.m.-noon.

If you're visiting Bar Harbor, bring the kids to the **Dorr Museum** (207-288-5395). Open Tuesday through Saturday, the natural history museum, which is located on The College of the Atlantic campus, is home to a tidepool tank, dioramas of coastal Maine wildlife, student exhibits, and natural objects for hands-on exploration. Admission to the museum is donation-based.

Kid Central Festival
Various locations, downtown Bangor
kidcentralfest.com

You have to love a citywide celebration that is purely dedicated to kids 12 and under. Visit for all kinds of creative activities, stories, face-painting, live music, and games. If your child is feeling inspired, there is also a superhero dress-up contest! The festival is free and open to the public. A full schedule of events is available on the website.

Can-Am Crown International Sled Dog Races, Fort Kent
Photo by Beurmond Banville

Summer

Few Mainers leave the state during summer—there is simply too much natural beauty to enjoy. Summer in Vacationland brings wildflowers, lush fields of grass, sparkling lakes to swim in, and miles of beaches to explore.

My family tries our best to soak up these dreamy Maine summer days until we're ready to slip back into the regular routine of fall.

On the  Water

One of the best parts about being in Maine is easy access to lake and ocean views from the shore. And while sitting at a scenic pier or swimming in a sparkling lake has its advantages, there is nothing better than seeing the landscape by boat on a clear summer day. Whether you board a schooner, paddle with a guide, or board a ferry, you are sure to enjoy views of islands, lighthouses, working lobstermen, and wildlife up close.

If you decide to take a daytrip on the water, always call ahead to check on pricing and availability. Summer is a busy time in Maine, so you'll want to reserve your space whenever possible.

Southern

Portland Schooner
Maine State Pier
Portland
(207) 766-2500
portlandschooner.com

My family celebrated a friend's birthday on the schooner *Bagheera*, a 1920s wooden vessel that sails for two hours on Casco Bay. The captain allowed the kids to take turns steering and let them explore below deck. We packed a picnic lunch and spent a picture perfect afternoon admiring views of Peaks Island, Fort Gorges, and **Bug Light Park** (see page 14). Sailing trips begin in May and run through October. The cost is higher

than other experiences on the water, however children 12 and under sail at a discount.

Portland Paddle
1 Cutter Street
Portland
(207) 370-9730
portlandpaddle.net/tours

Portland Paddle provides tours of the Casco Bay for varying ages and levels. Depending on the tour you choose, you might have the opportunity to see the lighthouses that dot the coast, impressive sailing vessels on the water, or historic forts, like **Fort Gorges** (pronounced gorgeous). Located on Hog Island, Fort Gorges was built in 1858 to protect Portland Harbor during

the Civil War. Portland Paddle offers guided, three-hour sea kayak tours for kids ages 10-16, where paddlers get to tour the abandoned fort and its mysterious hallways. You'll pay a higher price to paddle with a tour, but the opportunity to get up close and explore sites like Fort Gorges is unforgettable.

Peaks Island Ferry

Casco Bay Lines, 56 Commercial Street
Portland
(207) 774-7871
cascobaylines.com

Peaks Island is less than a 30-minute ferry boat ride from Portland. The ferry provides an inexpensive way for a family to get out on the water; tickets are free for children under 5. Once you arrive, explore the island by bicycle. Rentals are available from **Brad's Bikes** (207-766-5631). The loop around the island is a feast for the eyes—complete with pretty seaside cottages, oceanfront views, and rocky beaches to explore. My children also enjoyed a visit to the quirky **Umbrella Cover Museum** (207-939-0301), where musician Nancy 3. Hoffman entertains her guests with stories and music. Expect to spend a half-day on the island.

Milly's Skillet Seaside Kitchen, a food truck that makes its home at Jones Landing (Welch Street, Peaks Island), is perfect for a quick and satisfying lunch. For a refreshing treat after riding, visit **Down Front** (50 Island Avenue), a souvenir shop that serves Maine-made Gifford's ice cream.

Scarborough Marsh Audubon Center

92 Pine Point Road
Scarborough
(207) 883-5100
maineaudubon.org

Rent kayaks and canoes by the hour and explore the Dunstan River, where you'll likely spot sandpipers along the shoreline. Stop by the nature center to learn more about birds, shells, and native wildlife. Open Memorial Day through September.

Midcoast

Maine Maritime Museum Cruises

243 Washington Street
Bath
(207) 443-1316
mainemaritimemuseum.org/visit/cruises

The Maine Maritime Museum is a fun place for kids to explore any time of year, but I'm especially fond of their

cruises along the Kennebec River. There are several types to choose from, but for younger kids, the hour-long **Shipyards & Lighthouses Cruise** treats visitors to the history of the City of Ships. Best yet, the ticket price includes admission to the museum that's good for two days (within the same week).

Stop by **Mae's Café & Bakery** (maescafe-andbakery.com) in Bath for breakfast or lunch served all day. The warm, welcoming café is beloved by locals and travelers alike for enticing pastries and hearty meals that are sure to please even the pickiest of eaters.

Bufflehead Sailing Charters
Windjammer Wharf, Captain Spear Drive (off 50 Tillson Avenue)
Rockland
(207) 691-5407
sailrockland.com

The coast of Rockland is breathtaking, and the opportunity to sail the harbor is worth the investment. Tailored for families, *Bufflehead* can sail anywhere between an hour to a full-day (my family sailed 4 hours, which went by in a flash). Bring lunch and watch lobster boats haul traps, porpoises play in the water, and Bald Eagles soar above.

Cabbage Island Clambakes
22 Commercial Street
Fisherman's Wharf
Boothbay Harbor
(207) 633-7200

Take a scenic ferry ride to a private, family-owned island and experience a classic Maine clambake, complete with lobster, clams, corn on the cob, and roasted potatoes—all steamed seaside. There's plenty of green space for the kids to play, and bigs slabs of moist blueberry cake for dessert. Plan on paying a higher price than most outings, remembering that you get time out on the water plus a feast that will keep you full well past dinnertime. This is a great, all-ages trip your family will remember for years to come.

Lakes and Mountains

Songo River Queen II
Route 302/The Causeway
841 Roosevelt Trail
Naples
(207) 693-6861
songoriverqueen.net

Take advantage of this unique opportunity to cruise on a replica Mississippi Paddle Wheeler on Long Lake. The captain tells entertaining stories of the lake's history and points out loons and eagles along the way. You'll sail past Mount Washington and Pleasant Mountain, lakeside homes and summer camps. In case you forgot to bring snacks or lunch, there is food and drink to purchase on board. The cruise lasts 1 to 2 hours and is reasonably priced for families (kids under 4 ride free).

 If you want to bring lunch or a snack with you on the cruise, the **Good Life Market** (thegoodlifemarket.com) in nearby Raymond is my family's go-to stop for healthy food or take-out sandwiches.

Flagstaff Lake Scenic Boat Tours
Eustis Boat Launch (Route 27)
Eustis
(207) 246-2277
flagstaffboattours.com

The region around Flagstaff Lake is known for its unparallelled natural beauty. Jeff Hinman, a master Maine Guide, takes families on historic tours in his pontoon boat past incredible sights, including the Bigelow Mountain range, nesting Bald Eagles, loons calling on the lake, and maybe even a moose. For families, Jeff recommends a 4-hour tour, allowing time for the kids to swim on the beaches of **Bigelow Preserve**, which are only accessible by boat. Best for kids ages 8 and up.

Downeast and Northern

Northwoods Outfitters
5 Lily Bay Road
Greenville
1-866-223-1380
maineoutfitter.com

Families can book private trips with a registered Maine Guide to search for moose by canoe in the Moosehead Lake region. The guides, many of whom are parents themselves, know how to keep kids entertained and engaged. The moose tours last anywhere from 3 to 5 hours and run from May through October. Plan on paying a higher price for this special trip.

The Northern Outdoors
Old Canada Road Scenic Byway
1771 US Route 201
The Forks
855-968-3732
northernoutdoors.com

For children ages 8 and up, there is nothing quite like paddling the quieter part of the Kennebec River on two-person inflatable rafts called Duckies. Let the current gently carry you for a relaxing, 1- to 2-hour trip. The views of woods, vast water, and mountains are a delight.

Maine Coast Heritage Trust Trips
1 Bowdoin Mill Island
Topsham
(207) 729-7366
mcht.org

The Maine Coast Heritage Trust (MCHT), a conservation group that protects many of the state's coastal lands and islands, regularly sponsors affordable boating trips throughout the state—many of which are Downeast. Kids can explore remote islands, walk forest trails, and search for seaglass on the shore. Visit the MCHT website for a full trip schedule.

Lulu Lobster Boat
55 West Street
Bar Harbor
(207) 288-3136
lululobsterboat.com

More than 100,000 guests have enjoyed tours on *Lulu Lobster Boat*, where you can learn about lobstering while being treated to views of Egg Rock lighthouse, harbor seals, and Bar Harbor. You'll also hear fascinating stories, both real and legendary, about the area. Plan to tour for two hours. For kids 6 and up.

Where to  Swim

Whether you prefer freshwater lakes and ponds, or playing in the sand near the ocean, Maine has countless places to enjoy on a hot summer day. Many Maine beaches and lakes accept a **Maine State Park Pass** (see page 62), which allows entry to a park. Purchasing a season pass at a park entrance or maine.gov is a great way to save money, especially if you and your family hope to visit several state parks throughout the summer.

If you are planning a visit to the ocean or bay, be sure to check the tides by calling ahead or checking a daily tide chart for the area of your visit. Low tide can often mean more beach to enjoy at big ocean beaches. For bay areas and secluded coves, however, high tide can be more appealing. Wherever you plan to go, it's always best to ask first.

Southern

Winslow Park
Staples Point Road
Freeport
(207) 865-4198
freeportmaine.com

Winslow Park offers a modest beach on Casco Bay that's ideal for little ones, plus a playground that features a wooden pirate ship. During the summer months, there is a small fee to get into the park. Just be sure it's mid to high tide before you go (low tide can be mucky). In addition to being a fun place to swim, the park is also perfect for a cookout with friends. You'll find plenty of grills and picnic tables near the playground with a wide open view of Casco Bay. Winslow has a lovely, short walking trail through the woods with scenic views. The trail meanders along the Harraseeket River until it reaches Stockbridge Point. There is also a campground, but you'll need to reserve sites in advance.

Pine Point Beach (Hurd Park)
Pine Point Road and East Grand Avenue
Scarborough
(207) 730-4155
scarboroughmaine.org

If you're visiting Old Orchard Beach and the crowds at the beach are too

large, Pine Point, which is only ten minutes down the road, is a great option. The wide, sandy beach is great for building sandcastles or playing in the water. There is a small snack shack and a municipal parking lot nearby, too (Avenue 5, near King Street).

Crescent Beach State Park
109 Bowery Beach Road (Route 77)
Cape Elizabeth
(207) 799-5871
maine.gov/crescentbeach

Crescent Beach is one of my family's favorites for its expansive, sandy beach, ample parking, convenient changing rooms and a rotating cast of food trucks.

My kids love to explore the western end of the beach, where there are big rocks to scale.

Kettle Cove State Park
Kettle Cove Road (off Route 77)
Cape Elizabeth
(207) 799-5871
mainetrailfinder.com

Located just 2 miles away, Kettle Cove is part of Crescent Beach State Park. Parking is limited in this popular spot, so if you're able to find a free space, consider yourself fortunate. My family loves to bring breakfast, sit in the grassy area that rests above the beach, and search for hermit crabs in the tidepools below.

Kettle Cove, Cape Elizabeth

Long and Short Sands Beaches
Long Beach Avenue/US Route 1A
York Beach
(207) 363-1040
yorkparksandrec.org/attractions/beaches/

If you're looking for beaches that are in close proximity to York's popular shops and amusements, Long and Short Sands beaches are good choices. Be sure to go when the tide is out, when there is more beach to explore. There is no fee to visit, but be prepared to pay for street parking.

When my children were under 5, we made it a summer tradition to visit **York's Wild Kingdom** (yorkswildkingdom.com). I recommend spending the first part of your morning touring the impressive zoo, complete with tigers, monkeys, a petting zoo, and butterfly garden, followed by an afternoon at the amusement park. It's a full day, but always a treat for young families.

Footbridge Beach
Ocean Street
Ogunquit
(207) 646-2939
ogunquit.org

Expansive **Ogunquit Beach** is the most popular and best known in the area, but I like the quieter Footbridge Beach, which is located over the Ogunquit River. There is no fee to use the beach, but you do have to pay to park. If you don't pack a lunch, there is a modest snack shack serving hamburgers and hot dogs nearby. If you don't want to pay the high parking fees, take the **Ogunquit Trolley** (ogunquittrolley.com). The trolley offers designated stops throughout town, and the cost to ride is only a few dollars.

Drakes Island Beach
Foster Lane
Wells
(207) 646-2451
wellschamber.org

There are two other public beaches in Wells: **Wells Beach,** and **Crescent Beach**. I like Drakes Island Beach best for its soft sand and tall sea grasses. There is limited parking for a small fee, so get there early.

 Scoop Deck (scoopdeck.com) in Wells is a festive place to visit for ice cream after a day at the beach. It's hard to resist their big flavor board featuring creative flavors like Cinnamon Coffee Cake and Lemon Meringue Pie.

Goose Rocks Beach
Kings Highway (off Route 9)
Kennebunkport
(207) 967-1610
kennebunkportme.gov

Goose Rocks is beloved for its wide, white sand beach and walkable location, but whether you are local or from out-of-town, a visit requires some planning beforehand (Memorial Day through Labor Day). On the day of your visit stop by the parking sticker kiosk (Proctor Avenue and Kings Highway) or **Goose Rocks Beach General Store** (3 Dyke Road) for a day-use parking sticker (both locations are open on the weekend) or Kennebunkport Town Hall (6 Elm Street), which is open 8 a.m. to 4:30 p.m. Monday through Friday. If you're planning on a longer stay, you can visit any of these locations with a multi-day beach pass. To ensure a good parking spot, plan on getting to the beach in the early morning hours. It's worth the effort because at low tide, you can walk out to **Timber Island** and explore; just be sure to wear water shoes. There's a tide clock on the trailhead, so you'll know just what time to return back to land.

If you're unsure about walking to Timber Island, **Timber Point Trail** (www.tpl.org), which is located on Granite Point Road in nearby Biddeford Pool, connects to the island, and the trailhead is accessible by car. You'll find an easy 1.4-mile loop to walk. The spectacular scenery ranges from seaside homes and private beaches to a rocky coastline and open seas. You'll also discover an educational pollinator garden for kids and an abandoned summer home, which was built in the 1930s, along the trail.

Mother's Beach
Beach Avenue (off Routes 9 & 35)
Kennebunk
(207) 985-2102
kennebunkmaine.us

Mother's Beach is especially designed for parents with little ones. There is a beach parking kiosk on site, making it easy to grab a pass for the day. You'll also find a playground for added fun. And, in case you forgot to check ahead of time, there is still a fair amount of sand at high tide. On Beach Avenue, you'll discover two more beaches in walking distance, **Gooch's Beach** and **Middle Beach**.

Old Orchard Beach in Ocean Park
Temple Avenue
Ocean Park
(207) 934-9068
oceanpark.org

Old Orchard Beach (oldorchardbeach-maine.com) is popular for its nearness to amusements, fair food, and shops, but my family loves the quiet of this stunning, 7-mile section of beach in Ocean Park. There are parking spots available in town, plus an old-fashioned soda fountain within walking distance from the beach.

Ferry Beach State Park
95 Bayview Road
Saco
(207) 283-0067
maine.gov/ferrybeach

This peaceful state park is a family favorite for its tucked away feel. Park in the lot and take a short stroll down a wide boardwalk before you hit the soft sand and gentle surf. You'll also find a shaded picnic area, a nature center, and trails to explore.

If you're in Saco, a visit to **Funtown Splashtown** (funtownusa.com) is a must. The family-owned amusement/water park is small and easy to get around, making it a joy to visit. When my children were small, they loved the kiddie bumper boats and automated antique cars. Kids ages 7 and up will want to try an impressive wooden roller coaster called ExCalibur and making a splash on Thunder Falls, New England's tallest log flume. There's an old-fashioned sweet shop on site, which regularly has lines of visiting campers gripping bags full of homemade confections and kid favorites like Swedish Fish and Twizzlers.

Midcoast

Lincolnville Beach
US Route 1
Lincolnville
(207) 596-0376
camdenrockland.com

Lincolnville Beach is a small, half-mile beach located on the shores of the Penobscot Bay with views of Islesboro. This beach is ideal for families with young children looking for a quick and convenient place to play. Parking is available along US Route 1 or in a small lot next to the beach.

 My family likes to get morning pastries or sandwiches to go from **Dot's Market** (dotsinmaine.com), which is located just 0.3 mile away from Lincolnville Beach.

Barrett's Cove Public Beach
Beaucaire Avenue (off Route 52)
Camden
(207) 596-0376
camdenrockland.com

Maine's oceans can be chilly in the summer, and for this reason, I often seek out freshwater swimming. Barrett's Cove, on Megunticook Lake, is a scenic and quiet family destination. The water is warm, there are picnic tables and grills, easy parking, and you get fantastic views of Mount Megunticook. For older kids (6 and up), there's also an anchored diving float for big jumps into the water.

Reid State Park
13 miles from US Route 1 (Route 127S)
Georgetown
(207) 371-2303
maine.gov/reid

Reid is special because little ones can swim in the warm, saltwater lagoon at Griffith Head or play among the rocks and sand at Todd's Point. There are

Birch Point Beach State Park, Owls Head
(page 57)

changing rooms and picnic tables with grills if you plan to spend a full day.

Popham Beach State Park
Maine Route 209
Phippsburg
(207) 389-1335
maine.gov/pophambeach

Popham is beloved by families with kids of all ages for its vast beach that offers everything from warm tidepools to explore and rocks to scale to seaside views that bring a wonderful sense of calm. If you're spending the day, make time to visit nearby **Fort Popham** (maine.gov/fortpopham). Located just a mile from Popham Beach, the granite fort was created during the Civil War but never fully completed. Kids love to peer out the windows that overlook the Kennebec River, where they can spy seals or walk the long stone corridors.

Mitchell Field
1410 Harpswell Neck Road
Harpswell
(207) 833-5771
hhltmaine.org

This sandy beach located on Harpswell Neck offers over 2 miles of shaded walking and biking trails plus a

beautiful bandstand and the local community garden.

Thomas Point Beach
29 Meadow Road
Brunswick
(207) 725-6009
thomaspointbeach.com

There's a small fee to go to Thomas Point, but the beach offers daily deals during the summer, such as Thank You Mom Mondays, where moms get in free (check for more park specials on the website). Families love the beach on Thomas Bay, the well-appointed playground, generous parking, and picnic tables for lunch outdoors. The park is also home to a popular campground.

Damariscotta Lake State Park
8 State Park Road
Jefferson
(207) 549-7600
maine.gov/damariscottalake

The minute my family pulled into the parking lot, I was smitten with this state park. There's a picnic area shaded by trees, a sandy beach, and warm lake water to enjoy. You'll also find a convenient changing area for before and after your swim.

Birch Point Beach State Park

Birch Point Beach Road
Owls Head
(207) 236-3109
maine.gov/birchpoint

A long dirt road takes you to this private inlet, which is also known as Lucia Beach. You'll find convenient parking nearby, which makes it easy to carry chairs, coolers, and beach pails. This is lovely spot to beachcomb or climb rocks with your kids. There is also a shaded wooded area, where you'll find picnic tables and barbecue grills.

Pemaquid Beach Park

27 Beach Park Road
Bristol
(207) 677-2754
bristolmaine.org

Pemaquid is a dream for young families. The ¼-mile beach features clean white sand, beach roses in bloom, and a convenient shop that rents sand pails and floats. You'll also find changing rooms, showers, and a snack shack. Free admission for kids 11 and under.

Also located at Pemaquid Beach is **Beachcomber's Rest Nature Center** (coastalrivers.org). In July and August, the center offers free creative workshops for kids which feature treasure hunts, celebrations, and sand sculpture contests. Some workshops may require pre-registration, so check the nature center website in advance.

Lakes and Mountains

Moy-Mo-Day-O Recreation Area

Route 25 West
Limington
(207) 637-2171
limington.net/recreation.html

Once a campground for girls, this historic recreation area on Pequawket Lake is a hidden gem. For a low price per car, families of all ages can enjoy a 1,500-foot sandy beach with all of the fun day camp amenities—tennis, volleyball, horseshoes, walking trails, and a playground. Canoes and kayaks are available to rent daily, and there are camp grills and picnic tables, too.

Bresca and the Honey Bee at Outlet Beach

106 Outlet Road
New Gloucester
(207) 926-3388
brescaandthehoneybee.com

For a small fee, your family can swim at Sabbathday Lake, where you can also rent paddle boats and colorful floats. The beach is ideal for families because it's easy to keep an eye on everyone from the shore. For strong swimmers, there's also a dock for endless jumps into the water. The Snack Shack offers rich and super creamy homemade ice cream, which I believe is some of the best in Maine.

Range Pond State Park
26 State Park Road
Poland
(207) 998-4104
maine.gov/rangepond

This park was a childhood favorite for my husband, and for good reason. Range Pond is almost always warm and swimming in its calm water is a treat. There is a generous beach area for kids to play and changing rooms. We've also brought our own canoe to explore the pond.

Sebago Lake State Park
11 Park Access Road
Casco
(207) 693-6231
maine.gov/sebagolake

My family's go-to spot for years, Sebago is a vast lake surrounded by tall pines. The narrow beach spans the lakeside, but most families choose a shaded picnic table to place their coolers, towels, and beach bags. There's a big parking lot and a short walk to the beach, as well as changing rooms, a snack shack, and nearby playground. We like to arrive before lunch, grill hamburgers and hot dogs, and swim all day.

Highland Lake Beach
Highland Road
Bridgton
(207) 647-3472
brigdtonmaine.org

This pretty public beach with views of the White Mountains has a grassy area for play, plenty of shade cover, and restrooms. I also like that it is in walking distance to the town of Bridgton.

 You can never go wrong with a hearty lunch or coffee and pastries from **Beth's Kitchen Cafe** (bethskitchencafe.com), right down the road from Highland Lake Beach, in Bridgton.

Mount Blue State Park
187 Webb Beach Road
Weld
(207) 585-2347
maine.gov/mountblue

Mount Blue, one of Maine's largest state parks, offers so much to do all in one place—your family can picnic on the lush green lawn, swim in Webb Lake, play hide-and-go-seek on the playground, or rent boats to take out on the water. Plus the spectacular view of the Western Mountains makes this beach a gem.

Cathedral Pines Campground
945 Arnold Trail
Eustis
(207) 246-3491
gopinescamping.com

This private campground is also home to a free public beach on Flagstaff Lake. Take in awesome views of Bigelow Mountain while the kids swim. If that isn't enough to entice you, there is also a play area and picnic tables, making it easy to spend a full day.

Downeast and Northern

Sand Beach
Sand Beach Road
Stonington
(207) 367-2351
stoningtonmaine.org

Park roadside or walk to this magical island beach, where tall pines and boulders hug the coastline. A short path through the woods will take you to a quiet cove, which is especially stunning at sunset.

If you are exploring the **Blue Hill** peninsula, there are several resources for finding tucked-away coves, beaches and island trails for families to explore. The **Blue Hill Heritage Trust** (bluehillheritagetrust.org), **Island Heritage Trust** (island-heritagetrust.org) and **Maine Coast Heritage Trust** (mcht.org) all protect and maintain public lands in the region.

Lily Bay State Park
State Park Road
Beaver Cove
(207) 695-2700
maine.gov/lilybay

My family stopped at Lily Bay on a whim, and we're so glad we did. The park offers a lush grassy area, playground, sand beach and swimming on Moosehead Lake. We enjoyed our visit so much we decided to spend the night at the campground, where you can get a campsite on the water.

In the nearby town of Greenville, there is an old-fashioned soda fountain located inside **Harris Drug Store** (207-695-2921). My family visited after a hot hike up Mount Kineo and appreciated thick chocolate milkshakes with whipped cream and ice cream sodas served in frosty glasses.

Peaks-Kenny State Park
State Park Road
Dover-Foxcroft
(207) 564-2003
maine.gov/peaks-kenny

Anytime I mention Peaks-Kenny to local friends, the reaction is almost always, "I love that park!" It's hard not to fall for the crystal blue waters of Sebec Lake with its impressive view of Borestone Mountain. You'll also find a grassy picnic area, which makes for one of the prettiest lunch spots. The park offers family camping, too.

Echo Lake Beach
Echo Lake Beach Road (off Route 102 S)
Southwest Harbor
(207) 288-3338
nps.gov/acad

Sand Beach in Acadia National Park gets attention for its dramatic rocky coastline and mountain views, but only a few brave tourists swim in the frigid water. **Echo Lake** is an equally beautiful place to visit, plus you'll find limited parking, changing rooms and bathrooms, a sand beach, and much warmer water. **The Island Explorer Bus** (exploreacadia.com), a free shuttle bus for visitors to Acadia, stops here if you want to leave your car behind.

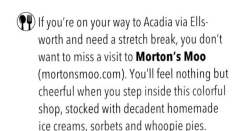 If you're on your way to Acadia via Ellsworth and need a stretch break, you don't want to miss a visit to **Morton's Moo** (mortonsmoo.com). You'll feel nothing but cheerful when you step inside this colorful shop, stocked with decadent homemade ice creams, sorbets and whoopie pies.

Lamoine Beach
Lamoine Beach Road
Lamoine
(207) 667-2242
lamoine-me.gov/parks.htm

While the beach is a mix of sand and pebbles, casually wading in Frenchman Bay on a hot day is a treat. This is a popular spot for picnicking with views of Mount Desert Island. **Lamoine State Park** (maine.gov/lamoine), which is located only 0.9 mile away, is an ideal spot for quieter family camping within easy travel distance to Bar Harbor and Acadia National Park.

Jones Pond
Recreation Road (off Route 195)
Gouldsboro
(207) 963-5589

If you want to avoid big summer crowds, Jones Pond is a great choice. This vast, 467-acre lake is located in the Schoodic Peninsula of Acadia National Park. Local families visit for the swimming in calm water and enjoy the day-use amenities, which include a playground, picnic area, and grills.

Roque Bluffs State Park
145 Schoppee Point Road
Roque Bluffs
(207) 255-3475
maine.gov/roquebluffs

I love a park with multiple swimming options. Roque Bluffs offers both saltwater (Englishman's Bay) and freshwater (Simpson Pond) swimming. Near Englishman's Bay, you'll find a stunning, half-mile pebble beach, where smooth stones and seaglass can be found. Families can also picnic, have fun on the playground, or explore the nature trails.

Portage Lake Public Beach
0.5 miles off Route 11
Portage Lake
(207) 435-4361
townofportage.org/recreation

If you're traveling to Aroostook County, this is a great spot for families to cool off, sunbathe on the lawn, or enjoy a picnic lunch. Kids can swim or enjoy the play area. A small campground is also located nearby (**Portage Lake Campground**, Portage Lake Boat Landing, West Road, Portage Lake, 207-435-4361).

Family Hikes+Outdoor Explorations

My family loves to get out and explore the woods during the summer months. Maine is home to a host of wildlife sanctuaries, nature preserves, and state and public parks. There are many options for beginning hikers, making it easy for families to explore some of the most beautiful parts of the state.

If you plan to see several parks and beaches throughout the season, a **Maine State Park Pass** is a smart choice. The pass affords your carload entrance every time you visit a state park. Visit maine.gov to learn how your family can purchase one. Passes can also be purchased at the entrance of most parks. For a nominal fee, kids might also enjoy a **Passport Book,** a pocket-size state park information guide that they can stamp when they visit a new park. Most passport stamping stations are located at the entrance. When kids collect several stamps, they are eligible for prizes that range from a free water bottle to free camping and even a free park pass.

Southern

East Point Sanctuary
Lester B. Orcutt Boulevard
Biddeford Pool
(207) 781-2330
maineaudubon.org

This short trail, which is less than a half-mile one-way, leads to an expansive field that's ideal for kite flying. Go just beyond the tall seagrasses, and you'll be treated to ocean views and rocks to climb. You may also spot the 19th-century **Wood Island Lighthouse** in the distance. Depending on your plans, you can spend a few hours or simply enjoy a relaxing walk. **Note:** There is parking for only six cars, so get there early in the morning if you can.

In July and August, **Friends of Wood Island Light** offer donation-based boat tours from nearby Vines Landing to Wood Island Lighthouse. Kids must be 10 and up to explore the steep steps in the tower. Visit woodislandlighthouse.org to reserve your space.

Rachel Carson National
Wildlife Refuge, Wells

Rachel Carson National Wildlife Refuge
321 Port Road
Wells
(207) 646-9226
fws.gov/refuge/rachel_carson

This easy 1-mile loop is especially good for little ones. The trail can accommodate strollers and there are plenty of stops along the way to admire winding tidal views and ocean vistas. There are also picnic tables on site if you want to bring snacks or lunch along. Plan on spending about an hour or two at the refuge.

Two Lights State Park
Two Lights Road (off Route 77)
Cape Elizabeth
(207) 799-5871
maine.gov/twolights

Kids love exploring the rocky shores of Two Lights while searching for snails and small crabs in the tidal pools. You can cook out using the park's charcoal grills and picnic tables all while taking in the deep blue waters of Casco Bay. There is also a playground near the parking lot and short walking trails that little ones might enjoy. Dogs on leash are also welcome.

Wolfe's Neck Woods State Park
426 Wolf Neck Road
Freeport
(207) 865-4465
maine.gov/wolfesneckwoods

Walk the short, shaded paths of Wolfe's Neck toward the shores of Casco Bay. During the summer, guides will help families spot osprey nests (May through August) from an oceanside overlook. There are four main trails, each totalling no more than 1.8 miles in length, including White Pines Trail, which is designed for strollers and wheelchairs. If you want to linger, plan on spending a few hours.

 Just down the road from the state park, you'll find **Wolfe's Neck Center** (wolfesneck.org), a 626-acre organic agricultural center where young families can visit with the animals, hop on a hayride, or rent bikes, kayaks, or canoes. Oceanfront tent sites and cottages are also available, should you want to stay for the weekend.

Midcoast

Giant's Stairs and McIntosh Lot Preserve
19 Ocean Street
Bailey Island
(207) 833-5771
harpswell.maine.gov

This 0.3-mile loop is made up of dramatic views of the Casco Bay, and you might catch glimpses of seals in the water. The Giant's Stairs were created by volcanic rock that eroded over millions of years. After a storm, you might also spot huge waves crashing against the shore. The loop finishes out another 0.2 miles along the McIntosh Lot Preserve—a small parcel of wild shrubland. Leashed dogs are welcome. If you plan to go off trail and traverse the rocks, wear good sneakers. **Note:** There are a few parking spaces available at the Episcopal Church just before the trailhead; alternately, bear right and you'll find two parking areas along Washington Avenue. When you visit, please respect this residential neighborhood.

Coastal Maine Botanical Gardens

132 Botanical Gardens Drive
Boothbay
(207) 633-8000
mainegardens.org

The highlight for families at CMBG is the **Bibby & Harold Alfond Children's Garden**. Spouting whales at the entrance and tiny cottages adorned with flower boxes make the garden look like a storybook come to life. There are areas dedicated to children's classics, like *Blueberries for Sal,* a treehouse to climb, a bear cave to explore, and a section of forest for fairy house building. Plan on spending a full day. **Note:** Free admission for Maine residents every Memorial Day weekend.

Fort Edgecomb

South off of US Route 1
Edgecomb
(207) 882-7777
maine.gov/fortedgecomb

This unique, octagonal blockhouse, which was built in the 1800s to protect the shipping center of Wiscasset, is one of the best preserved small forts in the nation and fun for all ages to explore. Located on the grounds of Wiscasset Harbor, Fort Edgecomb is also a scenic place to picnic with family.

Thomaston Town Forest Trail

Jack Baker Woods Trailhead
Beechwood Street
Thomaston
(207) 594-5166
georgesriver.org

A boardwalk path through lush, green woods leads you to **Split Rock**, a giant boulder that split in half during the last ice age (the walk is a little less than 2 miles round-trip). My family hiked on a rainy day, but we were well-protected by tree cover. The expanse of trees and large ferns lining the path looked like something out of the jungle. While hiking, my son dubbed the woods, "Maine's own Jurassic Park."

Beech Hill Preserve
Beech Hill Road (Summit Road Trail)
Rockport
(207) 236-7091
coastalmountains.org

A 0.6-mile one-way hike takes you uphill past fields of blueberries to a scenic overlook of Penobscot Bay and Camden Hills. A historic stone hut built in 1917 sits at the top. Pack a lunch and sit on the patio for a memorable afternoon. **Note:** In early August, the preserve opens for a few hours for wild blueberry picking.

Lakes and Mountains

Pleasant Mountain
Route 302 (past Shawnee Peak)
Bridgton
(207) 647-4352
loonecholandtrust.org

At 2,006 feet Pleasant Mountain is one of Southern Maine's tallest. The 1.8-mile one-way **Ledges Trail** (1,600 feet elevation) is a good option for climbers ages 6 and up. You'll find scenic overlooks along the way, and at the summit,

360-degree views of Moose Pond and the White Mountains. My kids left feeling like they made a big climb. For families looking for more options, the 10.5-mile trail system also offers a few longer hikes.

Sabattus Mountain
Sabattus Trail Road
Lovell
(207) 925-1056
mainetrailfinder.com

This mountain is a great choice if you're hiking with kids of varying ages (the youngest in our crew was three years old). At 1,253 feet, it's a quick 1.4 miles round-trip. The kids also had fun geocaching during this climb, and searched for hidden treasures along the trail.

Maine Huts & Trails
Kingfield
(207) 265-2400
mainehuts.org

If you want to hike and spend the night at your destination, a visit to Maine Huts & Trails is ideal. My family hiked a fairly flat and scenic 3.3 miles (one way) to Poplar Hut, one of four modern eco-lodges on the property. Meals are served at the huts for hungry hikers, and there are fire pits on the grounds for evening s'mores. Your family can also

Moxie Falls, The Forks

Debsconeag Ice Caves, T2 R10 WELS (near Millinocket), Photo by Rick LeVasseur

choose to stay a few days and hike from hut to hut for more woodland adventures. Before you go, call ahead to check availability or to reserve your spot.

Center Hill Nature Trail
Mount Blue State Park
299 Center Hill Road
Weld
(207) 585-2347
maine.gov/mountblue

The view of the Tumbledown and Jackson Mountains from the parking lot and picnic area is stellar, which makes this a satisfying, simple hike for kids. The half-mile loop brings you to glacier-carved ledges and a well-worn path surrounded by red oaks. At the top of Center Hill (1,640 feet) you'll find a small bog. There are a few steps to climb and a bench along the way to stop and take in the scenery. After your visit but before leaving the park, enjoy the swimming area at Webb Lake.

Downeast and Northern

Moxie Falls

Lake Moxie Road (look for State Park sign)
The Forks
(207) 623-4883
kennebecvalley.org

At 90 feet, Moxie Falls is one of the highest in New England. The 0.6-mile one-way trail to the falls is flat and easy to traverse with little ones and pets. Wooden overlooks let you view the waterfall from above. This popular trail is best to access in the morning hours to ensure parking.

Debsconeag Ice Caves

Debsconeag Lakes Wilderness Area
Ice Caves Trail
16 miles north of Millinocket on the Golden Road
(207) 729-5181
nature.org/maine

This adventurous trip, which is located near **Baxter State Park**, is best for kids 6 and up. Climb a gently sloped and heavily rooted trail for a mile (one-way) to two caves that were created during the last Ice Age. The first feels like a damp, dark cellar and the second cave, which has a steel-runged ladder to climb down, has a thick wall of ice covering the walls and floor. From the fork in the trail, walk just 0.2 mile more for spectacular views of First Debsconeag Lake.

Crockett Cove Woods

Fire Road 88
Deer Isle
(207) 729-5181
nature.org/maine

I was intrigued by this coastal forest, and it remains one of the most magical family walks in memory. Rich green moss and lichen cover the trees and rocks, and the soft, woodland trails are shaded and cool. Families can choose from three easy loop trails to explore.

🍴 If you're hiking in or around Deer Isle, bring your family to lunch at **El El Frijoles**, a California-style taqueria in Sargentville (elelfrijoles.com). The cheerful restaurant has outdoor seating and a play area, complete with a swingset and sandbox.

Crockett Cove Woods, Deer Isle

Acadia National Park, Park Loop
Bar Harbor
(207) 288-3378
nps.gov/acad

If you don't mind the crowds, the Park Loop is ideal for families of all ages. You can spend a few hours or a whole day exploring. My children and I walked **Sand Beach**, climbed the rocks and listened to the boom of waves crashing at **Thunder Hole**, explored the trails near **Otter Cliffs**, and then took a break at **Jordan Pond House** for lemonade and their famous popovers. Most sections of the Park Loop are well-marked and offer bathroom facilities. At Thunder Hole and Jordan Pond House, you'll find shops on site for snacks, drinks, and souvenirs.

After a break at Jordan Pond House, consider a drive up **Cadillac Mountain**—the highest point on the east coast. You and your family will enjoy dramatic views of coastal and inland landscapes.

If you've already enjoyed the Park Loop, consider seeing the park from a new perspective. Acadia National Park offers ranger-led programs throughout the summer into early fall, from boat trips to local islands to educational walks throughout the park.

Charlotte Rhoades Park
191 Main Street (Route 102)
Southwest Harbor
(207) 266-6047
rhoadesbutterflygarden.org

For parents with little ones who are looking for a quiet place to play or picnic, Charlotte Rhoades Park is the answer. Walk through the colorful perennial gardens, where you are likely to see butterflies fluttering about. The kids can play on the shaded lawn while you set up lunch on a picnic table overlooking Norwood Cove. In late July, the park is also home to an annual **Painted Lady Butterfly Release**. Tickets for this fundraising event are available on the park's website.

Farm Visits+
Berry Picking

One of the highlights of summer in Maine is the ability to experience so many unique area farms. Kids can meet local farmers, visit with the animals, enjoy the freshest homemade ice cream in the state, or pick berries.

If your family is planning a morning of berry picking, plan on getting to the farm early and consider the weather. Berry picking on an overcast or misty day to beat the heat is always a good idea. Be sure to call ahead to check on hours and picking status before you go.

Remember that working farms are often home to farming families. It's important to respect their hours, so as not to intrude with farm work or private life.

For families who are interested in getting to know local farms, **Maine Open Farms Day** takes place in July with farms open to the public. Check getrealmaine.com for details.

Southern

Spiller Farm
85 Spiller Farm Lane
Wells
(207) 985-2575
spillerfarm.com

Bring your own containers to fill with strawberries, raspberries, and blueberries at this no-nonsense berry farm (check the website for picking times).

Winslow Farm
291 Gray Road
Falmouth
(207) 878-8787
winslow-farm.com

Pick highbush, organic blueberries at a roadside flower farm where black-eyed susans and hydrangeas are in full bloom. The farm provides handmade wooden carriers for pickers, making it easy to carry pints brimming with berries.

Toots
137 Walnut Hill Road
North Yarmouth
(207) 829-3723
tootsicecream.com

Located in a little red caboose, Toots ice cream stand is beloved for their decadent homemade flavors, like Candy Store Floor and Grandma's Peanut Butter Fudge. While enjoying an ice cream, your family can spend time visiting the farm animals. You'll see everything from bunnies and goats to gargantuan cows and pigs.

Snell Family Farm
1000 River Road
Buxton
(207) 929-6166
snellfamilyfarm.com

This sweet, family farm offers pick-your-own raspberries, colorful perennials, and farm-fresh produce. After a morning of picking, kids can visit the small, man-made pond filled with frogs and lilypads.

Midcoast

Fairwinds Farm
555 Brown's Point Road
Bowdoinham

(207) 729-1872
fairwindsfarmmaine.com

Located on the banks of the Kennebec River, Fairwinds Farm is a lovely spot to pick strawberries. The farm also offers blueberry and raspberry picking in late summer.

Sheepscot General Store and Farm
98 Townhouse Road
Whitefield
(207) 549-5185
sheepscotgeneral.com

Visit this farm in the morning to pick organic strawberries, and then stop in the store for a mid-morning pastry or wholesome lunch.

Erickson Fields Preserve
164 West Street
Rockport
(207) 729-7366
www.mcht.org

This lush preserve was once a dairy farm, and is now home to a garden designed to feed those in need. Explore its quiet, 1.4-mile loop trail through fields and forest. Dogs on leash are welcome.

Crabtree's Blueberries, Sebago

Lakes and Mountains

Gillespie Farm
752 Mayall Road
New Gloucester
(207) 657-2877
pinelandfarms.org

Gillespie Farm (Pineland Farms Produce Division) is one of my family's go-to spots for strawberries. At the start of the season, the berries are bountiful and easy to pick. Visit in August for blueberry and raspberry picking too.

Crabtree's Blueberries
703 Bridgton Road (Route 107)
Sebago
(207) 787-2730
crabcoll.com/blueberry/homepage.html

I love Crabtrees for the blue metal buckets they provide for picking, which go kerplink, kerplank, kerplunk a la *Blueberries for Sal* as each blueberry falls into the bucket. There are several varieties of highbush blueberries to choose from, and the picking is consistently good.

Chipman's U-Pick Strawberries
32 Goodwin Road
Minot
(207) 998-2027
chipmanfarm.net

Local families love this eight-generation family farm for its picture-perfect strawberries. The farm also operates stands in Poland, Windham, Gray, and Raymond.

Goss Berry Farm
311 Elm Street
Mechanic Falls
(207) 346-6811
gossberryfarm.com

A charming, white farmhouse marks the entrance to this picturesque berry farm that overlooks the Western Mountains. Most families visit for their sweet, red raspberries, but the farm also offers strawberry and blueberry picking in late summer. Fresh peaches and strawberries are also available at their farmstand.

Crestholm Farm Stand and Ice Cream
167 Main Street
Oxford
(207) 539-8832

It may be located across the street from a casino, but this family-owned ice cream shop serves simple, delicious homemade flavors like sweet cream and maple walnut. Little ones will also enjoy meeting the llamas, goats, bunnies, and sheep.

Downeast and Northern

Stutzman's Farm Stand & Bakery
891 Doughty Hill Road
Sangerville
(207) 564-8596

Stutzman's is beloved by their community and it's easy to see why. Local families flock to the farm early in the summer to pick strawberries by the quart or pound. Their farmstand and bakery offers greenhouse vegetables, homemade breads, and fruit pies. In recent years, Stutzman's has become well-known for Sunday brunch (April through December) at their cafe, where families enjoy wood-fired breakfast pizzas topped with farm fresh eggs, seasonal vegetables, and herbs. Other menu highlights include stuffed french toast, local coffee, and bacon. While you're dining, enjoy live music and views of the fields.

Beddington Ridge Farm
1951 State Highway 193
Beddington
(207) 638-2664
beddingtonridgefarm.com

You'll want to make the trip inland to visit this scenic farm where you can rake wild blueberries in fields on Beddington Ridge. When you're done picking, the farm offers modern winnowing equipment to clean your berries. Just be sure to call ahead to let them know you're coming.

Peaked Mountain Farm
16 Ellery's Lane
Dedham
(207) 249-5002
peakedmountainfarm.biz

This wild blueberry farm is the first in the state to create a sanctuary specifically for native pollinators, such as bumblebees and monarch butterflies. Families can tour the blueberry and wildflower fields by appointment for a small fee from May through October.

Cooper Farm at Caterpillar Hill
Cooper Farm Road (just after scenic turnout)
Sedgwick
(207) 374-5118
bluehillheritagetrust.org

Forage for wild blueberries in July and August while enjoying dramatic views of Eggemoggin Reach, the islands of Penobscot Bay, and the Camden Hills. You'll also find several loop trail options totaling 2.5 miles round-trip. **Note:** If you go, plan on wearing long pants and protecting yourself with bug repellant as ticks can be prevalent.

Bright Berry Farm
4262 Kennebec Road
Dixmont
(207) 234-4225
brightberryfarm.com

Pick your own organic raspberries, blackberries, and highbush blueberries on 2 acres of this lush former dairy farm surrounded by hills and forest. As with many berry farms, call ahead, or check

Fairs +  Festivals

Carnival rides! Fair food! Parades! Fireworks! A Maine summer festival is one big celebration. If you live in Maine, you're bound to have at least one that you look forward to all year. And if you're from away, visiting a festival is a great way to get to know a local community while having a fun day out with your family.

Southern

Peony Festival
Gilsland Farm Maine Audubon
20 Gilsland Farm Road
Falmouth
(207) 781-2330
maineaudubon.org

My family kicks off summer (and the end of the school year) at this sweet festival. Go to enjoy saucer-size peonies in bloom, homemade ice cream, and garden-inspired activities. You can also explore the grounds where you'll find short trails through the woods and fields near the Presumpscot River estuary.

Cape Farm Alliance Strawberry Fest
Maxwell's Farm
Two Lights Road
Cape Elizabeth
capefarmalliance.org/strawberry-fest

Maxwell's Farm, a six-generation coastal berry farm, is home to the Cape Farm Alliance Strawberry Fest during the last weekend in June. Young and old visit for live music, homemade desserts, local crafts for sale, and tractor rides to the fields for berry picking.

South Berwick Strawberry Festival
Main Street
South Berwick
(207) 384-2989
southberwickstrawberryfestival.com

The historic town of South Berwick supports its local non-profits with this festive event. You'll find decadent treats like strawberry shortcakes and cheesecakes, but for families with multi-age kids, the real standout is all of the fun events. Little kids will enjoy the pony rides, a bounce house, and face painting, while bigger kids can scale a rock wall or listen to live music.

Yarmouth Clam Festival
Main Street
Yarmouth
(207) 846-3984
clamfestival.com

What makes this July food festival truly special is the small community that puts the event together. My family visits every year for the quirky parade, Lime Rickeys, slices of homemade pie from a local church group and beautiful Maine-made crafts. My kids also love the carnival rides, especially the Ferris wheel that provides a bird's-eye view of the whole festival.

Midcoast

Windjammer Days
Boothbay Harbor
boothbayharborwindjammerdays.org

Sailing vessels of every kind are the star of this week-long maritime festival. Kids especially love the festive lighted boat parade, meeting the dastardly Pirates of the Dark Rose (a Maine-based pirate troupe), and fireworks over the harbor. Best yet, most of the events are free!

Bath Heritage Days
Bath
bathheritagedays.com

The City of Ships knows how to throw a big festival. You'll find a host of free activities for little ones on the library lawn, including crafts, games, and face painting. For older kids, there are carnival rides throughout the weekend. The colorful community parade, which is one of Maine's largest, is full of floats and fun surprises (my children were thrown ice pops and sprayed with water on one particularly hot July 4).

Maine Lobster Festival
Rockland
(800) 576-7512
mainelobsterfestival.com

With its host of restaurants and shops, Main Street Rockland is worth visiting on its own. Add a Lobster Festival to the mix and your family is guaranteed to have fun. My family goes for the quirky events like crate races, which require running from one wooden crate to the next without falling in the water, a cod fish carry where kids in rain gear do their best to keep hold of a slippery fish, and a kids' lobster eating contest.

Union Fair and Maine Wild Blueberry Festival
Fairgrounds Lane
Union
(207) 785-3281
unionfair.org

I love a country fair that promotes contests that require "no specific skills other than the ability and desire to have fun." Kids and adults participate in a rooster crowing and hen-cackling competition, blueberry spitting contest, and a dress your own zucchini contest, just to name a few. The fair also hosts a day completely devoted to kids with scavenger hunts, farm animals, and a reduced entry fee for families.

Lakes and Mountains

New Gloucester Strawberry Festival
Congregational Church Vestry
19 Gloucester Hill Road
New Gloucester
(207) 926-3260
ngucc.org

This old-fashioned church festival is known for decadent homemade strawberry shortcake topped with vanilla custard from Hodgman's (a local business that's been making frozen custard since 1946). Sit at tables with red-checkered

Great Falls Balloon Festival, Lewiston
Photo by David Hill

tablecloths and listen to bluegrass music from the Berry Berry Good Band.

Great Falls Balloon Festival
Simard-Payne Memorial Park
(off Oxford Street)
Lewiston
(207) 370-8548
greatfallsballoonfestival.org

Kids can run around inside a hot air balloon or watch them take flight over Lewiston and Auburn. On Sunday morning, the festival also hosts a Family Fun Day with races, face painting, crafts, and performances for little ones.

Ossipee Valley Music Festival
Ossipee Valley Fairgrounds
291 South Hiram Road
South Hiram
(207) 625-8656
ossipeevalley.com

This four-day music festival bills itself as super family-friendly, beginning with free admission for kids 18 and under. In addition to listening to a variety of live music, including roots, Americana, country, and folk, kids can participate in weekend music or crafts workshops, or go tubing on the Ossipee River. Tent camping is also free.

Downeast and Northern

The Maine Whoopie Pie Festival
Main Street
Dover-Foxcroft
(207) 564-8943
mainewhoopiepiefestival.com

If your family craves chocolate cake sandwiches with sweet cream filling, best known as whoopie pies, this is the festival for you. Visit for all varieties of the official Maine State treat like coconut and orange creamsicle, plus a whoopie pie eating contest, crafts, rides, and games for the kids. Free for kids 12 and under.

Harbor House Flamingo Festival
Main Street
Southwest Harbor
(207) 244-3713
harborhousemdi.org

This sweet, three-day festival in Southwest Harbor celebrates flamingos and all things pink (flamingo lawn ornament designer Don Featherstone was a festival regular for 17 years). Check out the popular Flamingo Parade for all its feathery glory and the kids carnival in the town park.

Maine Potato Blossom Festival

Fort Fairfield
(207) 472-3802
fortfairfield.org

Drive to "The County" to see the expansive fields of potato blossoms, and stay a few days for this fun, community-wide festival. Families can canoe or kayak on picturesque Monson Pond, watch a rubber duckie race on the Aroostook River, or take part in an old-fashioned potato picking contest. Kids of all ages will also enjoy the live music, parade, and fireworks.

Ploye Festival and International Muskie Derby

Fort Kent
(207) 834-5354
fortkentchamber.com
fortkent-muskie.com

This two-part festival boasts the World's Largest Ploye. Made with buckwheat flour, the Acadian ploye is similar to a pancake or crepe. Festival goers can take part in making or eating the giant ploye, which is 12 feet in diameter! While you're there, don't miss the Fort Kent Muskie Derby, a competition to catch the biggest muskie, one of the most aggressive freshwater fish.

Maine Potato Blossom Festival, Fort Fairfield, Photo by Paul Cyr

Fall

Some would argue that autumn is Maine's most beautiful season. If the weather cooperates, fall days can treat you to vast blue skies, golden sunshine, and leaves in full regalia. This is the time of year when fall festivals and state fairs begin. The apple orchards come to life. Farm stands are brimming with pumpkins and brightly colored mums. My favorite activity, by far, is walking in the woods with my children. There's nothing like exploring a trail on a crisp autumn day as the leaves fall at your feet.

Family Hikes+Outdoor Explorations

I can't pinpoint when the need to explore started, but somewhere along the line, I fell in love with walking Maine's woods and trails. As a parent, I've learned to tailor our hikes to what the kids can manage best. We look for trails that feature something special—a boardwalk through the woods, a waterfall, public art, or an historic fort. These curiosities keep the kids interested, and while I'm not sure my two would admit it, I'm certain they've become fans of our hikes together.

Southern

Mount Agamenticus ♿
Big A Universal Access Trail
Mountain Road
York
(207) 361-1102
agamenticus.org

Named after a former ski area, the Big A Universal Access Trail, which is located at the summit of Mount Agamenticus, can be accessed by car. The well-groomed, 1-mile trail is designed to accommodate strollers, wheelchairs, and beginning mountain bikers. You'll find views of the Atlantic Ocean and the White Mountains with lookout points along the way. Kids will enjoy climbing the stairs to the viewing platform and walking the boardwalk trails through the woods. As an added bonus, a Learning Lodge is also near the trail. The lodge offers nature programs, crafts, and games through Indigenous Peoples Day.

🍴 If you're on your way to Mount Agamenticus and don't mind a grab and go lunch, visit **Flo's Hot Dogs** (floshotdogs.com) in nearby Cape Neddick. The little red hot dog shack, in operation since 1959, is best known for their secret relish, which is even more delicious when accompanied with mayo and celery salt.

Scarborough Marsh, Eastern Trail
130 Pine Point Road (parking entrance)
Scarborough
(207) 284-9260
easterntrail.org

Fort Williams, Cape Elizabeth

**Orange Mushrooms, Bradbury
Mountain State Park, Pownal**
Photo by Meghan Louise

Most people know Scarborough for its nearness to the beach and its convenient access to stores and restaurants along US Route 1. Many don't realize that the town is also home to Maine's largest saltwater marsh. This 8.4-mile portion of the Eastern Trail, from Scarborough to Saco, is a lovely place to walk or bike. The flat terrain is ideal for young cyclists and families with strollers. The trail through the 2,700-acre marsh takes families over a scenic bridge with views of birds and wildlife. Dogs on leash are also welcome.

Saco Heath Preserve
Route 112/Buxton Road
Saco
(207) 729-5182
nature.org/maine

This 1.2-mile trail starts in the woods and leads to a raised boardwalk that kids love. The boardwalk, which has planks in variegated hues, reaches a wide open space with views of the heath (a peat bog formed by two small ponds). The accessible and easy trail is a great way to introduce little ones to short hikes.

Fort Williams Park
1000 Shore Road
Cape Elizabeth
(207) 799-2868
fortwilliams.org

This popular park, which is also home to **Portland Head Light**, is a destination for many travelers during the summer months. My family likes to go in the fall when it's a little less crowded. We play soccer in the expansive fields or explore the Cliff Walk Loop that leads to the lighthouse. The walk, which is less than a mile, provides families with plenty of opportunities to admire the dramatic views of rocky coastline and sea. Fort Williams Park also recently developed a Children's Garden, which includes streams to explore, climbing structures, footbridges, a slide, and rocks to climb.

Bradbury Mountain State Park
528 Hallowell Road
Pownal
(207) 688-4712
maine.gov/bradburymountain

Bradbury Mountain is a favorite destination among local families for many reasons. You'll find a generous play area, picnic tables, and several options for hikes to the 484-foot peak, which offers a spectacular view in fall. My family likes the mile-long Northern Loop, which provides a gradual climb to the top. Dogs on leash are also welcome on the trails. If you're visiting for a weekend, the park offers group camping.

Pettengill Farm
Pettengill Road (off Bow Street)
Freeport
(207) 865-3170
freeporthistoricalsociety.org

Even with its close proximity to downtown Freeport, many visitors don't know about this historic saltwater farm, which encompasses 140 acres of fields and woodlands, apple orchards, and a salt marsh. A 200-year-old farmhouse, last occupied by avid gardener Mildred Pettengill in 1970, can also be found here. Cars are not allowed on the property, but the 12-minute walk to the farm down a dirt road is worth the effort (you can park near the welcome sign at the gate). Families will find 3.5 miles of trails to explore and plenty of space to play.

During the first Sunday in October, families can enjoy Pettengill Farm Day—complete with crafts, hayrides, and live music, plus a chance to tour the farmhouse. Visit Freeport Historical Society on Facebook for event details (facebook.com/historicfreeport).

Midcoast

Fernald's Neck Preserve
Fernald's Neck Road
Lincolnville
(207) 236-7091
coastalmountains.org

Fernald's Neck Preserve is a popular spot for swimmers during the summer months, but I like walking here in the fall when the mosquitoes are long gone. The trails, shaded by tall pines, are designed for easy walks (the longest hike is 1.8 miles). My family and I hiked to Balance Rock, which is like nature's version of the Leaning Tower of Pisa. While visiting, you'll spot Megunticook Lake and Maiden Cliff in Camden.

👀 **Maiden Cliff** is accessible through the trails at Camden Hills State Park (maine. gov/camdenhills). The 1-mile, moderate trail is best for kids with good climbing skills and stamina. At 800 feet, you'll see Megunticook Lake from a unique (and often windy) vantage point.

Penobscot Narrows Bridge/Fort Knox
740 Fort Knox Road
Prospect
(207) 469-6553
mainedot/fortknox

A visit to the Penobscot Narrows Bridge Observatory gives families the opportunity to see autumn leaves in full color and the Penobscot River from 42 stories above. Northern New England's fastest elevator takes you up. After, explore Fort Knox, Maine's largest historic fort, which was completed in 1869 to protect the Penobscot River Valley from British invasion. Families can roam through its granite passageways and underground stairs (bring a flashlight). Above ground, look for cannons and various outbuildings. There are picnic tables on site if you want to bring along lunch. The park closes for the season on October 31.

Moose Point State Park
310 West Main Street
Searsport
(207) 548-2882
maine.gov/moosepoint

Kids ages 3 and up will feel like big hikers on this level park loop path that's only 1.2 miles long. See the sparkling blue waters of the Penobscot Bay, rocky coastline, and tall groves of birches and pines. Families can take a break

at the playground, picnic tables, or many benches along the way. There are also steps down to the water for added exploring. If you're a pet owner, this is a great place to walk your dog on-leash.

🍴 If you're able, stop at the **Belfast Co-Op** (belfast.coop) before your visit to Fort Knox or Moose Point State Park. The store offers an impressive variety of Maine made goods, as well as soups and sandwiches to go.

Rockland Breakwater Lighthouse
Samoset Road
Rockland
rocklandharborlights.org

In the early fall, when the weather is still warm, treat the family to a walk at Rockland Breakwater Lighthouse (circa 1902). A popular spot among photographers for its dramatic granite walkway, kids ages 4 and up will enjoy the half-hour walk to the lighthouse (there are gaps between rocks which require some careful navigating and good shoes). From the observation deck, you can see boats in Rockland Harbor and Owls Head Lighthouse in the distance. The lighthouse is open Memorial Day through Columbus Day, depending on weather and volunteer availability. **Note:** There are no restrooms at the lighthouse, so plan accordingly.

Josephine Newman Sanctuary
Route 127 South
Georgetown
(207) 781-2330
maineaudubon.org

This quiet, 115-acre sanctuary has many curious spaces to explore—bluffs above the ocean, stonewalls crisscrossing the property, and reversing falls. Families can choose from three short trails, totaling a little over 2.5 miles. The shortest and simplest of the three, the 0.75-mile Horseshoe Trail, takes you to the ruins of a small cabin that sits high on a ledge, as well as a waterfall.

🍴 While you're visiting Georgetown, treat the kids to lunch or dinner at **Five Islands Lobster Company** (fiveislandslobster. com), located on a working wharf. Families can watch the lobster boats pull in and out of scenic Sheepscot Harbor. The menu incorporates classic lobster pound fare, as well as summer favorites including hot dogs and hamburgers. Five Islands also runs an ice cream shop that serves Portsmouth, New Hampshire-made Annabelle's Ice Cream. Open through Columbus Day weekend.

Lakes and Mountains

Shepard's Farm Preserve
121 Crockett Ridge Road
Norway
(207) 739-2124
wfltmaine.org/shepards-farm

The highlight of this 20-acre nature preserve in Norway is the towering sculptures by Maine-born artist Bernard Langlais, which are scattered throughout its open fields. Kids will enjoy searching for all six, which include an owl, a cat, and a totem named Mrs. Noah. Families will also find shaded trails throughout the woods, which are designed for walkers or mountain bikers.

🍴 If you're looking for breakfast or lunch in Norway, visit **Cafe Nomad** (cafenomad. com). The inviting Main Street cafe features a locally sourced menu that will appeal to everyone in the family.

Androscoggin Riverlands State Park
Center Bridge Road (off Route 4)
Turner
(207) 998-4104
maine.gov/androscogginriverlands

There are a variety of trails to explore at Androscoggin Riverlands State Park, but for kids I prefer the Homestead Trail. The 1.1-mile out-and-back trail takes you through dense forest and past the remnants of an old farmhouse, where kids can see the impressive stone framework of the former home. The trail leads to the banks of the Androscoggin River (there is also a convenient outhouse here). Walk past the first picnic shelter and follow the trail to the shore of the river. This is where you'll find one of Maine's prettiest picnic spots and a great place for kids to play. There is also a commemorative bench where you can sit and take in the rich colors of the autumn leaves reflecting off the water. Should you want to take a different way back, two trails totaling 1.5 miles—the Harrington Path and Old River Trail—also loop back to the parking area.

Rattlesnake Mountain
Bri-Mar Trail, 85 South (between Routes 302 and 11)
Raymond
alltrails.com

First things first: There are no rattlesnakes on Rattlesnake Mountain (in fact, there are no venomous snakes in Maine). The Bri-Mar Trail is popular with families as this 2.5-mile up-and-back hike offers views of Crescent and Sebago Lakes. While the trail is located on private property, the owners welcome visitors (parking is available for four to five cars). At the start, you'll walk through a meadow that leads to a wide trail into the woods. The trail gets more challenging as you climb, making this a good hike for kids 8 and up. The first overlook doesn't provide much of a view, but the sprawling lake views at the second lookout makes this hike worth the trip. **Note:** You'll find tree roots are common along the trail. Be sure to watch your footing as you walk.

Bald Mountain
Bald Mountain Road
Oquossoc
(207) 778-8231
maine.gov/baldmountain

From the trailhead to the summit, this mile-long, gradual hike has a big payoff. Kids will love climbing the viewing platform to see a bounty of red, gold, and orange leaves during peak foliage season (plus a fantastic view of Rangeley Lakes and the surrounding mountains). If you're lucky, you might also spot a moose or deer along the trail.

Coos Canyon, Byron

Coos Canyon
Route 17
Byron
(207) 364-3194
rivervalleychamber.com

Located just off the roadside, Coos Canyon is a great place to explore for all ages. My family pulled over planning to take a quick stretch break, and we spent close to an hour exploring the rocks and throwing stones into the water. The Swift River runs through the gorge, making for unique patterns and textures in the rocks. Some say it's also an excellent place to pan for gold.

The experts at **Coos Canyon Rock and Gift** (cooscanyonrockandgift.com), which is located right across the road, will show you how to pan for gold in the Swift River free of charge. If you plan to try prospecting on your own, the family-owned shop rents all the tools you need to find treasure.

Step Falls Preserve
Route 26 (Bear River Road)
Newry
(207) 824-3806
mahoosuc.org/hikes

A popular swimming spot in the summer for its natural water slides, Step Falls is equally enjoyable in autumn. The walk to the falls through the forest is just 1 mile round-trip, with the most challenging climb occurring at the base of the falls to the top. If your crew is willing to climb, the view of the brightly colored mountains is one to remember. **Note:** There is a small parking lot, so if you plan to visit the falls, get there early in the day. Parking on the road is not permitted.

 Step Falls is about a mile down the road from **Grafton Notch State Park** (maine. gov/graftonnotch). The park is home to Screw Auger Falls, a 23-foot waterfall that lies within a narrow gorge on the Bear River.

Downeast and Northern

Lamoine State Park
23 State Park Road
Lamoine
(207) 667-4778
maine.gov/lamoine

Located on the shores of Frenchman's Bay, this park is ideal for kids 10 and under. The mile-long Loop Trail begins at the Ranger Station near a large granite sculpture designed by German artist Roland Mayer. The wide, level path leads kids to a treehouse where they can take a break and play. If you're at the park during the season (through Oct.

15), you might also spot Larry the Lobster. Grab the green tag underneath Larry and claim a prize at the Ranger Station. Family camping is also available.

👓 The geometric sculpture at Lamoine State Park is just one of 34 granite sculptures located on the **Maine Sculpture Trail** (schoodicsculpture.org). The trail spans more than 273 miles in Downeast Maine and is a great way to discover town parks, trails, and preserves.

Gorham Mountain Trail
Acadia National Park, Park Loop Road (just past Thunder Hole on right)
Bar Harbor
(207) 288-3338
nps.gov/acad

This popular trail is approximately 2 miles long and doable for kids 5 and up. I like to visit in the late fall, when Acadia is quieter. The path offers stone steps to climb, cairns to mark the way, and plenty of spaces to take a short break. At the 525-foot summit, you'll be rewarded with sprawling views of Sand Beach and the Atlantic Ocean. **Note:** You'll find a convenient parking lot for trail access just past Thunder Hole on the right.

Aroostook State Park
87 State Park Road
Presque Isle
(207) 768-8341
maine.gov/aroostook

For older kids (9 and up) who are accustomed to more challenging hikes, a visit to Quaggy Jo Mountain and its twin peaks makes for a memorable fall trip. The steep climb to the North Peak, which is 2.25 miles round-trip, offers views of Echo Lake, Haystack and Scopan Mountains, and the town of Presque Isle.

Jasper Beach Park at Howard Cove
Port Road (Route 92)
Machiasport
(207) 255-4516
machiasport.org/points-of-interest

In September, when warm days are still possible, visiting a beach feels like a special treat. This pocket beach, made up of smooth, volcanic stones, is a memorable place to beachcomb with kids. The hypnotic sound of the water rushing between the stones is calming to all who visit.

🍴 **Helen's Restaurant** (helensrestaurant-machias.com) in Machias is known for its hearty diner-style meals and famous homemade pies (I'm partial to the chocolate coconut graham cracker).

Little Abol Falls
Baxter State Park, Park Tote Road/Abol Campground
Millinocket
(207) 723-5140
mainetrailfinder.com (trail information)
baxterstatepark.org (park rules)

There are hundreds of miles of trails to discover in Baxter State Park, which can be overwhelming to first-time visitors. Little Abol Falls trail, which begins at Abol Campground, is the perfect place to start with young children. The hike, which ascends gradually, is just over 1.5 miles round-trip. While walking, you'll spot the southwest side of Katahdin before reaching a brook that makes a 15-foot drop to a small pool below.

When you visit the Ranger Station near the Abol Campground parking lot, ask for a Children's Naturalist Adventure Pack. Available on loan, the packs include dip nets, binoculars, nature guides, a flashlight, compass, sketchpad, and crayons to use on the trail. These cool packs are available on a first-come, first-served basis, so hit the trail early if you can.

Farm Visits+
Berry Picking

Like any family, we love our traditions, and apple picking in the fall is one of our favorites. While we pick apples, we plan our cooking and baking projects—a chunky homemade applesauce, warm apple crisp, and apple pie with crumb topping. After picking, we buy donuts and a gallon of cider, gather around a picnic table and soak in all the sweet goodness a Maine orchard has to offer. Before you go, be sure to check farm hours and which varieties are available for picking; that way there won't be any surprises when you visit!

In mid-September, apple orchards throughout the state participate in **Maine Apple Sunday** (maineapples.org). Visit for orchard tours, special events, baked goods, wagon rides, and more family fun.

Southern

McDougal Orchards
201 Hanson Ridge Road
Springvale
(207) 324-5054
mcdougalorchards.com

This seventh-generation family farm and farm stand is run by Ellen McAdam and her husband, retired National Oceanic and Atmospheric Administration Captain Jack McAdam. In the fall, families visit for pick-your-own apples, sweet late-season raspberries, peaches, plums, and pumpkins. There's also a corn maze, a fairy house village, and miles of trails for families to explore. Before you leave, be sure to visit Captain Jack's famous Donut Shack, which is the place to go for bags of freshly made mini cider donuts.

Zach's Corn Maze
7 Colby Turner Road
York
(207) 475-7857
zachsfarm.com

Each year, Zach's creates a new 12-acre corn maze design. Families visit for hayrides, pumpkin picking, and the chance to spend an afternoon at a beautiful farm. After your visit, stop by the nearby farmstand for sunflower

Sweetser's Apple Barrel and Orchards, Cumberland Center

bouquets and seasonal veggies, including Zach's famous sweet corn. For older kids, the farm offers flashlight tag in the maze after 7 p.m.

Hansel's Orchard

44 Sweetser Road
North Yarmouth
(207) 829-6136
hanselsorchard.com

Located off a long dirt road, Hansel's Orchard offers a quiet pick-your-own experience where you can roam the orchard with your children free from crowds. Bring a picnic and spend a little extra time under the shade of their apple trees.

Sweetser's Apple Barrel and Orchards

19 Blanchard Road
Cumberland Center
(207) 829-6599
maineapple.com

While you can't pick fruit in the orchards, Sweetser's Apple Barrel offers visitors an education in apples. The roadside market is the place to find more than 50 popular and heirloom varieties throughout the season. A helpful sign tells you the flavor and origin of each variety, and the knowledgeable staff will guide you toward the right apples for eating or baking. During the fall season, you can also find a beautiful selection of pumpkins, gourds, and mums.

Midcoast

Rocky Ridge Orchard and Bakery

38 Rocky Ridge Lane (US Route 201)
Bowdoin
(207) 666-5786
rockyridgeorchard.com

Rocky Ridge Orchard gives you the option of pulling a little red wagon through the orchards or you can hop on a hayride. Kids will love playing on the barn swing and choosing a pumpkin after apple picking. My family also loves the homespun feel of the bakery, where there's all variety of donuts, including cider spice, pumpkin, and chocolate.

Hope Orchards

434 Camden Road
Hope
(207) 763-2824
hopeorchards.com

There's so much to like about Hope Orchards. Bring your own bags for pick-your-own or select pre-bagged apples at the stand. Try their cider—pressed each Friday of the season. In October, the orchard hosts fun events including a fall festival with music, local food and crafts, and a weekend celebration of late fall apple varieties.

Beth's Farm Market

1986 Western Road
Warren
(207) 273-3695
bethsfarmmarket.com

This beloved Midcoast market is a fun stop for families. Beginning in September, kids can take a tractor hayride to the corn maze, for a fee, or try climbing a "mountain" made of 500 hay bales. Visitors can also pick apples, or purchase apples, pumpkins, and cider at the market. And while it's typically a summer treat, the homemade strawberry shortcake, made with sweet late-season strawberries and topped with whipped cream, is not to be missed.

Sewall Organic Orchard

259 Masalin Road
Lincolnville
(207) 763-3956
sewallorchard.com

There are few orchards that can boast a view like this one. At 900 vertical feet above sea level on Levenseller Mountain, visitors will spot Camden Hills State Park, Megunticook Lake, the foothills of Western Maine, and even views of Acadia. Enjoy their organic apples (available for purchase only) and reward yourself with a cup of freshly pressed cider.

Bailey's Orchard
255 North Hunts Meadow Road
Whitefield
(207) 549-7680

Pick your own fruit or shop inside the big, beautiful barn for up to 50 varieties of apples throughout the season. You'll also find pears, pumpkins, fall flowers, and gourds to take home. In addition to picking, kids will see how apples are turned into cider using a cider press.

Lakes and Mountains

Thompson's Orchard
276 Gloucester Hill Road
New Gloucester
(207) 926-4738

This popular orchard is known for their homemade donuts and apple dumplings, so be prepared for longer lines (I suggest visiting early in the season). Despite the crowds, local families go year after year for tractor rides, great picking, and the opportunity to spend an afternoon in a picturesque location.

Libby and Son U-Picks
86 Sawyer Mountain Road
Limerick
(207) 793-4749
libbysonupicks.com

This pristine, 40-acre orchard is nestled in a valley near Sawyer Mountain. Visit in early September and if the conditions are right, you can pick apples, blueberries, late-season raspberries and peaches. Kids will especially enjoy the golf cart rides out to the orchards. After picking, treat yourself to an apple smoothie or pumpkin donut with cream cheese frosting. The orchard also regularly hosts live music and sells hot lunch on the weekends.

 If you want to plan a daytrip, begin with a morning hike on the **Smith Trail at Sawyer Mountain** (fsht.org) in Limerick. This 2.4-mile round-trip hike requires stamina and is best for children 9 and up. My family is especially fond of the yellow turtle trail markers.

Wallingford's Fruit House
1240 Perkins Ridge Road
Auburn
(207) 784-7958
wallingfordsorchard.com

Wallingford's holds a special place in my heart. My husband grew up in Auburn and visited the orchard every fall with his family and introduced it to me when I first came to Maine. Now operated by Ricker Hill Orchards in nearby Turner (rickerhill.com), Wallingford's is located on a rural road with a scenic overlook. If you go, be sure to stop in the sweet-smelling bake shop for homemade sugar donuts and warm apple dumplings with vanilla ice cream.

 After a visit to Wallingford's, my family likes to walk the **Spring Road Trail** (mainetrailfinder.com) around Lake Auburn. It's a scenic walk with a wide trail that's suitable for even the littlest of hikers.

Pietree Orchard
803 Waterford Road
(between Routes 93 & 35/37)
Sweden
(207) 647-9419
pietreeorchards.com

This tucked away orchard, owned by author Tabitha King, offers an impressive selection of pick-your-own apples in fields that overlook the White Mountains (just be sure to call ahead to check picking conditions). The farmstand and store is also a wonderful resource for seasonal vegetables and fruit grown in their fields. If you're visiting during lunch time, be sure to save room for the homemade wood-fired pizza, and cider donuts for dessert.

Heritage Farm
1062 Auburn Road
Peru
(207) 562-7780

This roadside farm has homegrown pumpkins at a great value. Kids love searching among the rows to find the perfect pumpkin to take home for Halloween. The farmstand, which operates on the honor system, also sells squash, tomatoes, and fall vegetables.

Downeast and Northern Maine

Treworgy Family Orchards
3876 Union Street
Levant
(207) 884-8354
treworgyorchards.com

This fourth-generation family farm creates an impressive corn maze every year with designs ranging from knights conquering dragons to the world's largest tractor. In addition to the maze, families can also pick apples and pumpkins in the fields, tour the farm on a tractor-drawn hayride, or visit the petting zoo.

In late October, Treworgy Orchards hosts a ticketed Night Maze event, where families can bring their own flashlights and explore the maze under the stars. This event is designed with the youngest kids in mind—backlit trick or treating stations are set up throughout the maze.

Johnston's Apple Orchard
Branch Pond Road (off US Route 1A)
Ellsworth
(207) 667-4028

Families return to Johnston's year after year for a healthy variety of pick-your-own apples (and the price is excellent, too). Kids will enjoy exploring between the rows of trees in the sweetly scented orchards.

Thunder Road Farm
185 Newport Road
Corinna
(207) 278-2676
thunderroadfarm.com

I like Thunder Road Farm because their corn maze is designed for both little ones—there's a 15-minute section—and older kids, who can opt for an hour-long adventure. Young children will also want to check out the cow train, jumping pillow, pirate ship, and a barnyard ball toss. Before you go, stop by the farm-stand across the street for pumpkins and seasonal veggies.

Johnston's Apple Orchard, Ellsworth
Photo by Patrick Lessard

Goughan Farms, Caribou

Goughan Farms
875 Fort Fairfield Road
Caribou
(207) 498-6565
goughanfarms.com

Goughan's (pronounced "gone's" here in Maine) makes delicious homemade ice cream and is home to a variety of fun activities for the whole family—from an impressive corn maze and pick-your-own pumpkins to miniature golf, a petting zoo, and hayrides. The farm store also stocks gourds and mums for fall decorating.

Fairs+  Festivals

There is no better way to celebrate the beauty and bounty of fall than visit to a community festival. It's a treat to spend time outside all while learning about Maine food and farms. There's often a chance for kids to make autumn-themed crafts and play outdoor games. Many fairs host farming competitions, highlight local bands, and sell locally made crafts and food. With so much to see and do, a fall festival is an opportunity to enjoy a day out together, no matter how old your kids are.

On **Maine Open Lighthouse Day** (lighthousefoundation.org), a September event, lighthouses are open to the public for free throughout the state. The event provides an excellent opportunity to learn about the history of some of Maine's most iconic lighthouses, as well as a chance to explore their towers. Just be sure to wear your climbing shoes, as tower rungs can be steep.

Maine Craft Weekend (mainecraftweekend.org) takes place during the first weekend in October. Families have the opportunity to visit artists' studios and galleries statewide, watch artists at work, sample local foods, or try a new craft or art project.

Southern

Capriccio: Festival of Kites
Ogunquit Beach, Beach Street
(off US Route 1)
Ogunquit
(207) 646-2261
ogunquitperformingarts.org
The Festival of Kites is a part of a town-wide, two-week celebration of the arts. Kids can design their own paper kites (available for free) by the beach. Then, everyone is invited to join the Grand Kite Ascension, when dozens of unique kites take to the skies. Prizes are awarded to young participants for their creativity.

Cumberland Fair
Cumberland Fairgrounds
Blanchard Road
Cumberland
(207) 829-5531
cumberlandfair.com

I'll be honest—my kids go to the Cumberland Fair for the carnival rides. For me, the quieter parts of the fair, which are located opposite the carnival, are best.

I love sampling hand-pies, pulled pork sandwiches, and funnel cakes from local food trucks, seeing the award-winning pumpkins, and visiting the Sugar Shack for maple cotton candy. There's a host of fun events for everyone in the family, including a pig scramble and harness racing. Free admission for kids 12 and under. **Note:** Visit on one of three designated bracelet nights, typically Monday, Wednesday, and Thursday, where kids can enjoy unlimited rides for one price.

The Pumpkin Event
Spring Brook Farm & Market
168 Greely Road
Cumberland
(207) 829-5977
sbfarmandmarket.com

This bucolic, family farm is home to an ever-growing market and in late October, the farm opens its fields to visitors for pumpkin picking. Take a horse-drawn wagon ride to choose your own, and then return back to the market for homemade treats. Little ones will also enjoy a hay bale climb and bouncy house. Admission price includes wagon ride and your pumpkin.

Maine Apple Day Celebration
Gilsland Farm Audubon Center
Falmouth
(207) 781-2330
maineaudubon.org

This event is designed for children up to the age of 8. Kids can learn how to press cider, play nature-based games, take a woodland story walk, and listen to live bluegrass music. This celebration gets a little bigger every year—local food trucks now join in the festivities.

Camp Sunshine Pumpkin Festival
L.L.Bean, 95 Main Street
Freeport
(207) 655-3800
campsunshine.org

When you sponsor a pumpkin at this festival, the proceeds go to Camp Sunshine—a retreat center that supports children experiencing life-threatening illnesses and their families. At the event, kids can play fall-themed carnival games and get small prizes in return. At night, the L.L.Bean campus glows with the light of thousands of jack o' lanterns, including a tower of pumpkins with heart-shaped carvings.

Beast

Rolling Slumber Bed Races
Park Row
Brunswick
(207) 729-4439
brunswickdowntown.org

I ask you, where else can you see grown-ups racing down the street in themed costumes and coordinating beds? This free event, which features local businesses and nonprofits running for bragging rights, is guaranteed to make you smile. Before the race, a business group offers barrel train rides and a church organization has a bounce house for little ones.

Fall Foliage Festival
Boothbay Railway Village
586 Wiscasset Road
Boothbay
(207) 633-4727
railwayvillage.org

This traditional fall festival has something for everyone in the family. Kids will love exploring the historic outbuildings and the chance to ride a 100-year-old narrow gauge steam engine. Parents will also like browsing the craft fair with artisans from all over Maine. If that weren't enough, there's live music and giant pumpkin carving demos, too. Free admission for kids 12 and under.

Boothbay Railway Village

Damariscotta Pumpkinfest & Regatta

Main Street + various locations
Damariscotta
(207) 677-3087
mainepumpkinfest.com

During this three-day festival, Main Street in Damariscotta is lined with giant pumpkins decorated by local artists. Young families will also want to visit Saturday's mini fair with games where little ones are awarded points that they can exchange for small prizes. There's also a pumpkin derby, a pie eating contest, and a dramatic 600-pound pumpkin drop at Roundtop Farm, a local nature preserve with picnic tables and trails to explore. On Columbus Day, check out the regatta in Damariscotta Harbor, which features paddlers competing in huge hollowed-out pumpkin boats.

 While there's no shortage of pumpkin-flavored desserts at Pumpkinfest, my family prefers to visit **Round Top Ice Cream Stand** (207-563-5307) in Damariscotta for generous scoops of rich, homemade ice cream. I like the chocolate peppermint ice cream best, but many people go for fall-inspired flavors like Indian pudding and apple cinnamon.

Nobleboro Applefest

Nobleboro Central School
194 Center Street
Nobleboro
(207) 563-5376
nobleborohistoricalsociety.org

This old-fashioned Maine festival has entertained families since 1978. There are activities to keep the kids busy, including face painting and a climbing wall. Like any good community festival, there are a variety of tempting foods to try—homemade donuts, apples and cheeses from Beth's Farm in Warren (see page 100), and apple pies made by local families.

Common Ground Country Fair

294 Crosby Road
Unity
(207) 568-4142
mofga.org

Common Ground Country Fair, a three-day celebration organized by Maine Organic Farmers and Gardeners Association, attracts upward of 60,000 people each year. With that in mind, plan on arriving early (traffic through the small town of Unity can cause heavy delays). For kids 6 and under, a creative children's area offers a natural crafting tent and performance stage. Don't miss the whimsical Garden Parade, which features kids of all ages dressed in fruit- and veggie-themed costumes. Families will also enjoy seeing the farm animals ranging from rabbits and chickens to large draft horses and oxen. The farmers' market—one of Maine's largest—is worth a visit for organic vegetables, fresh flowers, and provisions from all over the state. For adults and older children, set aside time for the craft fair, which has hundreds of handmade items. Free admission for kids 12 and under.

The Youth Enterprise Zone on Friday and Sunday is a great choice for thoughtful gifts, homemade treats, and creative goods made by kids ages 11 and up.

Lakes and Mountains

Pineland Farms Harvest Festival
15 Farm View Drive
New Gloucester
(207) 650-3031
pinelandfarms.org

Pineland Farms is a bucolic place to visit, complete with rolling hills, forest paths to explore and an expansive market with a focus on Maine-made foods and gifts. The farm offers excellent children's programming throughout the year, but my family's favorite is the harvest festival.

Play outdoor games, including a farmers' obstacle course, explore an expansive corn maze, and experience an interactive woodland story walk where kids meet costumed characters along the way. For older children (10 and up) and brave adults, the farm comes to life at night with a Haunted Walk through the woods.

Shawnee Peak Fall Festival
119 Mountain Road
Bridgton
(207) 647-8444
shawneepeak.com

There's nothing quite like a chairlift ride to the top of Shawnee Peak in the fall. While the ride is a highlight, families also visit for live music, cider donuts, and fun activities for the kids. Admission is free for children 5 and under.

Bluegrass Festival
Apple Acres Farm
363 Durgintown Road
Hiram
(207) 625-4777
appleacresfarm.com

This certified organic apple farm is home to a lively and family-friendly bluegrass festival in late September. Visit for the music, and stay to pick your-own-apples. The farm also oper-

Pineland Farms, New Gloucester

ates a warm and inviting restaurant with outdoor seating that serves stone-fired pizzas. Take time to shop the farm store with locally produced syrup, honey, cheeses, decadent fudge and homemade pies. While you're visiting, relax and enjoy apple cider donuts, then let the kids have fun at the playground.

Fryeburg Fair
1154 Main Street
Fryeburg
(207) 935-3268
fryeburgfair.org

Maine's largest agricultural fair, which has been entertaining families for more than 165 years, is home to show horses, oxen, steer, and so much more. Don't miss the contests, including a skillet throw and a sweet baking competition for parents and kids. Little ones will enjoy the petting zoo, farm museum, and crafts area. For nursing moms, there's a convenient Mother's Lounge.

Bethel Harvest Festival
Town Common
Bethel
(207) 824-2282
bethelharvestfest.com

If you're searching for a beautiful day out with family, head to the Bethel Harvest Festival. While you're there, experience a horse-drawn wagon ride through town or visit the farmers' market. You'll also find activities for the kids, music to enjoy, crafters, and a chowder cookoff.

 While you're in Bethel for the festival **Sunday River** offers scenic chairlift rides. or visit **Gibson's Apple Orchard** (207-836-2702) which is also located in town.

Downeast and Northern

Eastport Pirate Festival
Various locations throughout Eastport
(207) 853-4343
eastportpiratefestival.com

If you have a kid who loves pirates, this three-day festival is for you. The coastal town hosts a big boisterous parade and fireworks at night. Little ones will like the pirate puppet show or watching pirates duel with swords, or if they're brave, they can visit a Pirate Encampment and learn what life is like at sea.

Machias Bay Harvest Fair
Station 1898
(Machias Bay Chamber of Commerce)
Two Kilton Lane
Machias

This annual community fair has a little something for everyone. A pumpkin chucking contest into the Machias Bay with homemade catapults and trebuchets is a highlight because really, where else can you see a contest like this? The event also features an area of local farmers and makers, which provides a great way to take something home that's uniquely Maine. Visitors can also enjoy live music and performers throughout the day. This family-friendly portion of the event is free (a ticketed wine and beer tasting happens late in the day).

In addition to the festival, two more events are held the same day—an annual 2-mile **Color Dash** (a non-competitive run/walk) that kicks off at University of Maine Machias fitness center (machias.edu) and ends at Station 1898, and a **Fly-In** at Machias Valley Municipal Airport (Airport Road, Machias), where families can see unique helicopters and aircraft on display. Flights are also offered by local pilots for a donation.

Blue Hill Fair
Route 172
Blue Hill
(207) 374-3701
bluehillfair.com

This beloved, five-day fair was the inspiration for the E.B. White classic, *Charlotte's Web*. The animals and crafts exhibits are a joy to visit for all ages. My family likes the Sunday afternoon women's skillet toss competition, horse and ox pulls, and a wild blueberry pie eating contest. Kids will also enjoy the demolition derby (think Matchbox cars come to life). If you have the opportunity to go on Thursday, adult admission is $1. Free admission for children 12 and under every day.

Acadia Night Sky Festival, Mount Desert Island
Photo by Ray Yeager

Acadia Night Sky Festival

Various locations
Mount Desert Island
(207) 288-5103
acadianightskyfestival.org

Celebrate the beauty of the night sky with a weekend of fun events. While there are some events geared toward younger children, such as an outdoor movie night in downtown Bar Harbor's Agamont Park, this festival is best for kids 10 and up. Visit for Night Sky parties, including a ranger-led tour of Sand Beach (bring glow sticks to keep track of your crew in the dark). Families can make star-themed crafts together and view constellations from the top of Cadillac Mountain.

 Right around the time of the Night Sky Festival, it's also Smithsonian Magazine's annual Museum Day Live! event. Visit smithsonianmag.com/museumday for two free tickets to the **Abbe Museum** (abbe-museum.org) in Bar Harbor. I love this small museum for its thoughtful exhibits on local native American tribes. The annual Waponahki Student Art Show, which highlights the mixed media work of school age children ages 3 to 18, is inspiring for kids and adults alike.

Scarecrow Festival

Various locations
Fort Kent
(207) 834-5354
fortkentchamber.com

This sweet celebration of autumn is held in conjunction with University of Maine Fort Kent's homecoming weekend. The highlight is most certainly the Saturday morning parade, where harvest floats and scarecrows of all shapes and sizes line the streets. You'll also find hayrides and fall-themed activities for the kids at **Bouchard's Country Store** (207-834-3237). The Bouchard Family (ployes.com) is well-known in Fort Kent for their ploye mix—a nutty, buckwheat flatbread that was once served by Acadian families at every meal. To learn more about this local delicacy, visit Fort Kent during the summer months for the Ploye Festival (see page 83).

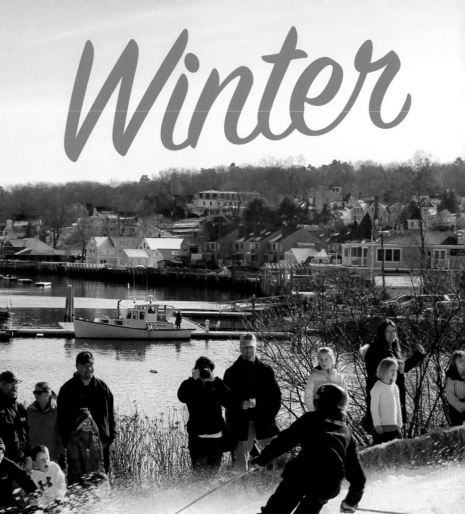

Winter

There's a celebratory feeling in the air when an early December snow arrives in Maine. If the sun is shining, the hills and evergreens glisten as if sprinkled in fairy dust. The arrival of the holidays add to winter's magic with hometown celebrations and festivals happening all over the state. At January's arrival, it's tempting to want to hunker down until spring, but I've learned the more time spent outdoors, the better my family's spirits. Maine is a virtual winter playground, offering beautiful natural spaces to ski, sled, and skate. Parents with little ones can start with small adventures, with cozy stays in cabins and yurts, visiting winter festivals with friends, and taking short snowshoe hikes. As children grow older, a family day spent snowshoeing, skating, or skiing becomes possible. And no matter your age, there's nothing more fun than a winter road trip to check out a place that's new to you.

Cross-Country Skiing, Snowshoeing+ Sledding

This is the time of year for sliding and gliding your way through farms, woodland trails, and seaside preserves. There are great options nearly everywhere you travel, whether it be a local golf course that opens up to sledding and cross-country skiing or a state park with groomed trails. Keep in mind that farms and preserves often ask for a donation or trail usage fee. Before your visit, it's always best to check websites or call ahead for usage fees, hours, and trail conditions. If your family enjoys both Nordic and downhill skiing, many area ski resorts also offer options for both (see the Downhill Skiing + Tubing section, starting on page 132) for more.

Southern

Wells Reserve at Laudholm
342 Laudholm Farm Road
Wells
(207) 646-1555
wellsreserve.org

If you have your own snowshoes or cross-country skis, the Wells Reserve is a lovely place to explore. The woodland and shoreline trails require a little more effort (they're not groomed), so this trip is best for older, more experienced kids. In February, the reserve hosts a Winter Wildlife Day where families are invited to sled on the grounds and enjoy hot cocoa.

Harris Farm
280 Buzzell Road
Dayton
(207) 499-2678
harrisfarm.com

At the 500-acre Harris Farm—a fourth generation dairy and vegetable farm—nearly 25 miles of groomed trails at varying levels take skiers through rolling pastures and peaceful woodland paths. Parents can rent sleds to pull little ones along. Skate skis, snowshoes, and Nordic skis, boots and poles, and fat tire bikes are also available to rent. It's free for kids 6 and younger, which is ideal if your children are new to Nordic skiing. The farm also offers private and group lessons. After skiing, warm up in the lodge near

Harris Farm, Dayton

the woodstove. You can pack lunch or, on weekends, the farm sells hot dogs, snacks, and warm drinks. Be sure to stop by the farmstand for a bottle of flavored milk. Creamy and velvety smooth, Harris Farm chocolate milk is the best I've ever tasted.

Smiling Hill Farm
781 Country Road (Route 22)
Westbrook
(207) 775-4818
smilinghill.com

Enjoy 15 miles of groomed ski trails at this historic dairy farm. Skis, boots and poles, pulk sleds, and snowshoes are available to rent, and kids younger than 6 ski for free. The dairy store offers ice cream, cheeses, and flavored milks, plus a straightforward lunch menu featuring soups, sandwiches, and mac and cheese. It is open year-round should you want sustenance after your ski.

Riverside Golf Course
1158 Riverside Street
Portland
(207) 797-3524
trails.org

Part of the Portland Trails system, the city-owned Riverside Golf Course offers more than 4 miles of groomed trails for snowshoeing and cross-country skiing. The golf course is also a popular place to sled and ice skate during the winter months. If you're hungry after a morning of skiing, the Riverside Grill, also located on the grounds, is open for lunch.

While rentals are not available at Riverside Golf Course, families can borrow a limited number of snowshoes in advance from **Portland Trails** (305 Commercial Street; trails.org) with a membership. Call (207) 775-2411, Monday-Friday 10 a.m. to 4 p.m.

Val Halla Golf and Recreation Center
60 Val Halla Road
Cumberland
valhalla.golf

Located at the end of a residential road, Val Halla is a peaceful spot to snowshoe or ski with family. The trails are groomed, but plan to bring your own equipment. Local families also flock to this spot for sledding.

 Sprawling **Twin Brook Recreation Area** (185 Tuttle Road), also in Cumberland, offers nearly 6 miles of groomed trails for cross-country skiers. Bring your own skis.

Midcoast

Hidden Valley Nature Center
131 Egypt Road
Jefferson
(207) 389-5150
midcoastconservancy.org

Hidden Valley has nearly 15 miles of groomed trails in a scenic woodland setting, including a gentle loop around Little Dyer Pond (bring your own skis and snowshoes). There's even a warming hut available for after your ski. The center is also home to an insulated cabin for winter stays; just be prepared for a 2-mile trek with your gear. For younger skiers who want the experience of a wintertime visit, there is a yurt and a rustic hut on site that's less than half a mile, one way, from the parking area.

Camden Hills State Park
280 Belfast Road (US Route 1)
Camden
(207) 236-0849
maine.gov/camdenhills

This state park is well maintained in the winter and is a popular spot for cross-country skiing and snowshoeing. Families will find snow-packed trails

to explore that are well-marked for easy exploration. For skiers, the 5-mile one-way, multi-use trail begins at the main entrance to the park and leads to the Megunticook Ski Shelter, which can be reserved for overnight stays. Families with little ones might enjoy the 0.3-mile, one-way Shoreline Trail with views of the Penobscot Bay.

Oak Point Farm
60 Samoset Road
Boothbay
(207) 633-4818
bbrlt.org

Explore one mile of field and forest trails at this saltwater farm located on Hodgdon Cove. Your family will traverse over small bridges, around a large freshwater pond, and past heirloom apple trees. The gentle terrain is perfect for all ages, as it varies from flat to a gradual slope. You'll find an 18th-century farmhouse on the property (home to the Boothbay Region Land Trust) where there is convenient parking and restrooms available Monday through Friday. Bring your own snowshoes or skis.

Lakes and Mountains

Pineland Farms
15 Farm View Drive
New Gloucester
(207) 688-6599
pinelandfarms.org

Pineland Farms (see page 110) is an ideal place for families during the winter months. For cross-country skiers, snowshoers and even fat tire bikers, there is a rental center with everything you need. The well-groomed trails are 19 miles in all. Along the way, you will find outdoor firepits with marshmallows to roast. If skiing isn't your family's thing, there is also an impressive sledding hill (sleds are also available for day-long rentals), winter disc golfing, and a skating rink. After your time outdoors, stop by the Welcome Center and Market for hot drinks, baked goods, or soups and sandwiches.

🔭 If you're in the area and looking for a memorable winter stay, **Maine Forest Yurts** (maineforestyurts.com) in Durham is the ideal place. The yurts, which were created by "Survivor" winner Bob Crowley, his wife Peggy and their family, are heated by a woodstove, offer a full kitchen, bunk beds and futons. Bring your snowshoes, explore the grounds, and skate on Runaround Pond. Dogs are also welcome.

Five Fields Farm
720 South Bridgton Road (Route 107)
South Bridgton
(207) 647-2425
fivefieldsski.com

For a unique, cross-country skiing experience, try this picturesque, hilltop orchard, where you'll find nearly 13 miles of trails to explore with a view of Mount Washington in the distance. Equipment rentals are available in the farmstand. Five Fields welcomes dogs and snowshoers. Adventurous older kids who don't mind a climb might be interested in hiking backcountry trails 20 minutes to the top of nearby **Bald Pate Mountain** (loonecholandtrust. org), which abuts the farm. There's also a cozy warming hut for after your ski.

Carter's Cross Country Ski Center
786 Intervale Road
Bethel
(207) 824-3880
cartersxcski.com

Carter's is where I tried nordic skiing for the first time. I instantly fell for the trails among farm fields with their majestic mountain views. Cross-country ski, fat bike and snowshoe rentals (kids under 6 are free) are available. You'll find a variety of woodland and open

Carriage Trails, Acadia
Photo courtesy of Friends of Acadia/Julia Walker Thomas

trails for all levels of skiers. Carter's is dog-friendly, should you want to bring along your furry friend. Just be sure to call ahead. They also offer off-the-grid cabin rentals for extended stays.

Roberts Farm Preserve
64 Roberts Road
Norway
(207) 739-2124
wfltmaine.org

This 165-acre nature preserve features 10 miles of groomed trails for cross-country skiing. Roberts Farm is especially ideal for kids who are new to the sport, as trail use is free. A warming hut,

which is open on weekends and school holidays, has equipment on loan for guests. Visitors will also find trails for snowshoeing and winter dog walking.

In mid-February, the town of Norway celebrates a **Snowshoe Festival** (wfltmaine.org) to commemorate snowshoe inventor, fiddler, and Norway resident, Mellie Dunham. The town-wide event includes snowshoe races at Roberts Farm, games for kids, a snowshoe tug-of-war, and the Snowshoe Wife-or-Whatever Carry.

Quarry Road Trails
300 Quarry Road
Waterville
(207) 314-0258
quarryroad.org

If you're searching for a simple place to cross-country ski, sled, or snowshoe, Quarry Road is a good choice. The 200-acre park has more than 6 miles of groomed trails to explore and snowmaking capabilities to help extend the season. Snowshoers can traverse the wooded walking trails that follow along the banks of Messalonkee Stream, and sledders can slide down the old Colby ski hill. There is also a lighted section of the trail for nighttime exploration. At the Welcome Center Yurt, families can purchase day passes or rent skis for a small fee (free for kids 6 and under). Snowshoes are free of charge.

Downeast and Northern

Holbrook Island Sanctuary State Park
172 Indian Bar Road
Brooksville
(207) 326-4012
maine.gov/holbrookisland

This 1,230-acre nature preserve, which was donated to the state in 1971, is a peaceful place to explore on snowshoes or cross-country skis. The trails take you through forests and shoreline and around ponds and marshes. Keep in mind that the terrain is not groomed, so the sanctuary is best for older children. Families can also enjoy skating on Fresh Pond, a shallow pond that's often clear of snow due to the sanctuary's proximity to the coast.

Acadia Carriage Road Trails
Acadia National Park
Mount Desert Island

The carriage road trails, which were constructed by John D. Rockefeller Jr. in 1915, are a popular place to bike in Acadia National Park during the summer and fall. But in the winter, after the crowds have long gone, the wide trails—with their views of lakes, waterfalls, and ocean, are even more spectacular. Local volunteers groom nearly 30 miles of roads when new snow is above 6 inches, and visitors are welcome to ski or snowshoe on designated trails. While the Eagle and Upper Hadlock loops are often groomed first, families prefer the Witch Hole Pond trail for its easy accessibility and length (the trail is 3 miles round-trip). **Note:** Ski conditions change hourly, so be sure to check the **Friends of Acadia** (friendsofacadia.org) Facebook page (https://www.facebook.com/FriendsofAcadia) for updates.

Caribou High School Ski Center

Caribou High School
308 Main Street
Caribou
(207) 551-0022
mainetrailfinder.com

A friend of mine grew up in Caribou, and she told me one of the great benefits of living in town is its easy accessibility to cross-country skiing. Case in point: The high school has nearly 2 miles of lighted trails, so families can ski for free at night (there's an additional 1+ miles of trails for daytime skiing). There are also snowshoeing trails that follow a spring through the forest. And if that weren't enough to impress you, the high school even has a lodge to gather in after your ski. Bring your own skis or snowshoes.

Nordic Heritage Center

Off Fort Fairfield Road (Route 167)
Presque Isle
nordicheritagecenter.org

This ski center, whose red buildings stand out emphatically in the snowy landscape, has more than 22 miles of trails. You'll find a trail for every level of skier (my family of beginners likes the Moose Trail with views of Katahdin). Fat tire biking trails are also on site. Ski and snowshoe rentals are available, and pet owners will find a dog-friendly ski and snowshoe loop. After venturing outdoors, warm up in the lodge.

Fort Kent Outdoor Center

33 Paradis Circle
Fort Kent
fortkentoc.org

The Fort Kent Outdoor Center plays host to some of the best skiers in the world, but don't let that intimidate you. The center is also an impressive space for recreational skiers who are looking to explore the northernmost corner of the state. When you arrive, you'll find a lodge that is home to a full-service cross country and snowshoe shop, where you'll also find rentals and day passes (free for kids 6 and under). Warm up at the Waska Loop, which is a little less than a mile long, or bring the kids to the nearly 3.5-mile Violette Settlement Trail loop. The center also has designated snowshoe trails, dog-friendly ski trails, and a sledding hill near the parking area and main lodge.

Ice  Skating

In Maine, there are so many options for skating, indoors or outside. Children can bring along friends and spend an hour or two gliding—or sliding—across the ice. Just be sure to call ahead to check on ice times and conditions.

Southern

The Waterhouse Center
51 Main Street
Kennebunk
(207) 604-1335
kennebunkmaine.us/facilities

This covered open-air skating center can be found right in the heart of Kennebunk. Bring your own skates and enjoy the feeling of skating on clean, outdoor ice day or night. Skating is free. **Note:** Rink parking is shared with the Kennebunk Village Pharmacy.

If you're visiting the Waterhouse Center and are looking for a special treat or warm drink after your skate, stop by **Boulangerie** (aproperbakery.com). The tiny, tucked-away bakery and cafe is home to flaky croissants, crisp chocolate chip cookies and simple, pre-prepared baguette sandwiches.

The Rink at Thompson's Point
10 Thompson Point
Portland
(207) 222-3031
therinkatthompsonspoint.com

The covered outdoor rink at Thompson's Point is located off I-295 on the bank of the Fore River. Admission to the rink is higher than at other local skating venues, but its unique location and delicious local offerings make it a fun place to visit. There are skate rentals available if you don't have your own, as well as skating aids for little ones who are just learning and a Polar Bear Skate Pond, a beginner rink for kids under the age of 12. Food trucks, hot drinks, a warming yurt, bar (for parents), and a lounge are also on site.

When the weather isn't cooperating, the indoor **William B. Troubh Ice Arena** (portlandmaine.gov) also offers public skating.

Falmouth Family Ice Center
20 Hat Trick Drive
Falmouth
(207) 781-4200
familyice.org

The Falmouth Family Ice Center is a local favorite, as families can rent skates (free for children under 5) and skate on the large indoor rink during designated hours or skate outdoors on Lee Twombly Pond. On days when the temperature rises above 25 degrees, my family typically chooses the pond. There's a warming hut with picnic tables, benches, cubbies for gear, and a fieldstone fireplace. Families are welcome to bring lunch or snacks along. There are also lights around the pond for evening skating.

Orland H. Blake Skating Pond
188 Main Street
(parking behind Key Bank)
Yarmouth
(207) 846-2406
yarmouthcommunityservices.org

This quintessential New England skating pond is where my children learned to skate. There is a warming hut with a wood-burning fireplace and benches, where you can store your gear underneath. BYO skates and ice time is free. Yarmouth Community Services (200 Main Street, behind Town Hall) offers free skates to borrow and return, Monday through Friday, 8:30 a.m. to 4:30 p.m.

Scarborough Ice Rink
20 Municipal Drive
Scarborough
(207) 883-7645
scarboroughmaine.org

This generous outdoor rink is divided into two sections—one for simple skating and another for pick-up games of ice hockey. Visitors will also find an indoor area to put on your skates (bring your own).

Midcoast

The Brunswick Mall Ice Rink
Lower Mall Park, Maine Street
Brunswick
(207) 725-6656
brunswickme.org

Brunswick is home to three ice rinks, but the mall rink, which is located in a tree-lined park at the town center, is a favorite for its generously sized outdoor rink. Bring your own skates, and for kids looking to play ice hockey, check the website for designated hours. Skating is free.

Goddards Pond
High and Marshall Streets
Bath
(207) 443-8360
bathrecreation.com

This lighted skating pond is a beautiful place to go for an evening skate, and if the temperatures drop, there is a warming hut for your comfort. You'll find a little concession stand with warm drinks and goodies, just in case you forgot to pack snacks. **Note:** This is a natural pond, so a green sign indicates when conditions are safe for skating.

Round Top Farm Community Ice Rink
3 Round Top Lane
Damariscotta
(207) 563-1393
coastalrivers.org

Round Top Farm, a 12-acre preserve that includes a Victorian-era farmhouse and historic barn, is a beautiful place to visit any time of year. The addition of the outdoor rink makes it even more special. The rink is free for anyone to use; just bring your own skates or hockey equipment. Helmets are also required for safety for kids under 18. The volunteer-run warming hut, which is open on weekends only, has hot chocolate available to skaters.

Midcoast Recreation Center
535 West Street
Rockport
(207) 236-9400
midcoastrec.org

When the weather isn't cooperating, this indoor rink serves as a great option for families. Skating passes and rentals are also reasonable. The rink regularly hosts learn-to-skate sessions and fun events during the winter months.

Lakes and Mountains

Norway Savings Bank Arena
985 Turner Street
Auburn
(207) 333-6688
norwaysavingsbankarena.com

This great big indoor arena is Maine's first and only dual-surface arena, which means there are two rinks available for skating. There are open ice times for all levels of skaters. Rentals and skating passes are also available for one a flat fee.

Androscoggin Bank Coliseé

190 Birch Street
Lewiston
(207) 783-2009
www.thecolisee.com

Lewiston, which is a town with a strong Franco-American heritage, is home to an indoor ice *coliseé* (French for coliseum), which hosts concerts and sporting events. There is also public ice time throughout the season for families. Skates are available to rent. The Coliseé is also home to some special events for little ones, including Skate with Santa, in December.

Bruce Fox Memorial Ice Rink

Cottage Street
Norway
(207) 743-6651
norwaymaine.com

I love the little community of Norway, and this lighted town rink adds to its charms. If you don't own skates, there are some available at the rink to try for free. There's also a warming hut to enjoy after your time on the ice.

Mount Blue State Park Ice Rink

Center Hill Road (Ranger Station)
Weld
(207) 585-2261
maine.gov/mountblue

This beloved local rink, which is located in Mount Blue State Park (see page 58, summer), is known for its extensive views of the Western Mountains. There are donated skates available in case you forget to bring your own and a warming hut for before and after your skate. Mount Blue is also home to a sledding hill, groomed trails for cross-country skiing, snowshoe, and snowmobile trails.

In early February, celebrate Family Fun Day at Mount Blue State Park. Families can learn about winter camping and fat tire bikes, experience a winter nature walk, or go on a hay ride. The Maine Bureau of Parks and Lands (parksandlands.com) has skis and snowshoes available to try for free, and hot lunch is served (for a nominal fee) to all who visit.

Chalmers Ice Arena

Bridgton Academy
36 Hancock Drive
Bridgton
(207) 647-3322, ext. 1310

This indoor rink, which is also known as Bridgton Ice Arena, offers reasonably priced public skating for families throughout the year (with the exception of April, May, and June). Skates, as well as stick and puck rentals, are also available to guests.

Downeast and Northern

Penobscot Ice Arena
90 Acme Road
Brewer
(207) 989-7183
penobscoticearena.org

Sunday afternoon skating is a hit at this indoor arena, where music plays while you glide on the ice. All levels of skaters are welcome and skates are available to rent. Check the website for other public skating and Stick & Puck times.

Sawyer Ice Arena
107 13th Street
Bangor
(207) 947-0071
bangorparksandrec.com

This city-owned arena, which is located in Hayford Park, is known for its NHL-sized rink. Families can enjoy public skating during the week and weekends. Admission is reasonably priced. Bring your own skates.

Glen Mary Park
11 Waldron Road
Bar Harbor
barharborvia.org

This community pond, tucked away in a residential neighborhood, is part of a public park operated by the Village Improvement Society. The quiet, tree-lined park is an ideal place to bring little ones who are just learning to skate. Bring your own skates.

Chris's Pond
Chris's Lane
Southwest Harbor
(207) 244-5404

If you're searching for a quiet, community pond to skate on, Chris's Pond is the perfect place. Local volunteers keep the pond clear throughout the season. Bring your own skates or, if your older children are willing, take part in a game of pick-up ice hockey.

The Forum
84 Mechanic Street
Presque Isle
(207) 764-0491
pirec.org

For families, this local rink is a gem. Parents will appreciate the convenient group rate for skating, inexpensive skate rentals, and the availability of skating aids and sleds for little ones. You'll also find a snack bar in case you need some sustenance after an afternoon on the open ice.

Downhill Skiing + Tubing

The options for downhill skiing are plentiful in Maine, especially for families. Many mountains offer specially priced tickets and lessons. For moms and dads who love to ski, but have a baby in tow, several resorts also offer day care options. And if that weren't enough to entice you, more and more resorts are also providing tubing, which is a fun alternative if you're visiting with a group that's made up of non-skiers and skiers.

Midcoast

Camden Snow Bowl
20 Barnestown Road
Camden
(207) 236-3438
camdensnowbowl.com

The Snow Bowl is known for its small-town feel and as the only Maine ski resort with ocean views from its summit. A friend says visiting this ski area is like tailgating at a sporting event—many families come with their own picnic supplies and stay for the day. Families will find a conveyor carpet lift for young skiers, a rail park for tricks, and night skiing. Best yet, kids 5 and under can ski for free with a paying adult.

The Camden Snow Bowl is also home to a circa 1936 **Toboggan Chute** with 440 feet of wooden track. It's a fast,

heart-pounding experience that lands brave riders on a vast frozen pond below (plan on sliding a few extra feet once you hit the pond). Riders must be at least 42 inches tall to use the chute, which is open on weekends and school holidays. Just be sure to call ahead to check conditions.

Lakes and Mountains

Lost Valley
200 Lost Valley Road
Auburn
(207) 784-1561
lostvalleyski.com

Lost Valley is a local favorite for beginning skiers and snowboarders. The modestly sized mountain offers eight beginner trails and modestly priced lift tickets, and has a big lodge with a snack bar for you to enjoy during your visit.

On weekends, families can try the snow tubing park. Lost Valley is also home to nearly 5 miles of groomed Nordic ski trails, showshoe trails, and fat tire biking trails.

Seacoast Adventure
930 Roosevelt Trail (Route 302)
Windham
(207) 892-5952
seacoastadventure.com

This snowtubing park is conveniently located off Route 302, making it an easy stop for a quick weekend adventure. Kids will like that there's a lift to the top, so there is no need to walk tubes up and down the groomed 700-foot hill. In the evenings, the park lights up the hill and there is a fire pit to keep everyone warm. Parents will appreciate the onsite coffee shop, where there is also hot cocoa for the kids. For safety reasons, kids between 3 to 4 feet tall need to ride in a double tube with an adult.

Seacoast Adventure, Windham
Photo by Ginny Davis

Sunday River ♿

15 South Ridge Road
Newry
(207) 824-3000
sundayriver.com

It's hard to believe that this wildly popular resort began as a community ski mountain. Today, Sunday River is made up of 870 acres encompassing 135 trails and eight different peaks (if you go, plan on a meet-up spot after your ski). For beginners, there are 41 different trails to choose from. Many choose the South Ridge, where all trails are beginner and most are lighted for night skiing. This section is also home to the Snow Sport School, retail stores, ziplines, and dining. The Dreammaker Trail, which is located on the North Peak, is a family favorite for its long, wide descent. Older kids will also find an award-winning terrain park on this peak and the younger set will like meeting Eddy the Yeti in his Enchanted Forest home.

Though Sunday River has the most expensive lift ticket in Maine, the resort offers a variety of amenities. Near the South Ridge Lodge, there's a day care for kids 6 weeks to 6 years, as well as combined day care/learn-to-ski packages for 3- to 4-year olds. Sunday River also supports **Maine Adaptive** (maineadaptive.org), a free program that provides kids with physical disabilities (ages 4 and up) the opportunity to ski and snowboard with trained volunteers.

Shawnee Peak

119 Mountain Road
Bridgton
(207) 647-8444
shawneepeak.com

Shawnee Peak first opened in 1938, which makes it the longest operating ski resort in the state. It's also home to the most night skiing in New England. Families with new skiers will find seven beginner trails and two magic carpets—a conveyor-style lift that transports little ones up the hill with ease. A day care on site is also a nice plus for parents with kids under 6. From the top of Shawnee, skiers will enjoy views of Moose Pond and the New Hampshire Presidential Range. Two lodges offer food and drink options. For local families, Shawnee Peak is known for its active after-school program, which offers lift tickets at a reasonable rate. During February break, the mountain is home to a three-day adventure camp, where kids 7 to 12 get personal instruction, lunch and the opportunity to play games and ski freestyle.

Black Mountain, Rumford
Photo by Nancy Charlebois

Sugarloaf ♿

5092 Access Road
Carrabassett Valley
1-800-THE-LOAF
sugarloaf.com

At 4,237 feet, Sugarloaf is Maine's second highest peak after Mt. Katahdin. It's also the largest ski resort in Maine. That said, newcomers to the sport shouldn't be intimidated. Sugarloaf offers a variety of lessons for skiers of all ages. Like Sunday River, its sister resort, you'll find several options for beginners on Double Runner and West Mountain. There is a magic carpet lift for little ones and five terrain parks for older kids, plus options for childcare. Like Sunday River, Sugarloaf is a sponsor of **Maine Adaptive** (maineadaptive.org), a program for children ages 4 and up and adults with physical disabilities.

On days when the weather isn't cooperating, families can take advantage of the **Anti-Gravity Center Complex** (207-237-5566), which is located at the base of the mountain. The complex includes an indoor skate park, rock climbing wall, trampolines, and a gym.

Sugarloaf is also home to an impressive Outdoor Center (207-237-6830), which provides options for Nordic skiing, snowshoeing and fat biking on 56 miles of groomed trails, plus its own Nordic ski lodge. Families will also love the NHL-sized skating rink. And if you purchase a lift ticket to Sugarloaf, you get full access to all, including equipment rentals.

Mt. Abram

308 Howe Hill Road
Greenwood
(207) 875-5000
mtabram.com

Much like Lost Valley in Auburn, Mt. Abram is a popular place for local families who are just learning to ski. Skiers will find smaller crowds than at the larger resorts, making for a stress-free day of skiing with family. The Westside of the mountain is known for its great landscape for learning and has its own lodge (parking is limited here, so take the shuttle from the Main Mountain parking lot). On the Westside, families will find a double lift and magic carpet.

Black Mountain of Maine

39 Glover Road
Rumford
(207) 364-8977
skiblackmountain.org

Black Mountain is made for families looking for skiing and other winter activities at a reasonable price. Most impressive is that K-2 graders can ski for free all season long. You'll also discover a well-designed lodge with downhill skis, snowboards, and Nordic ski rentals (the mountain also offers over 10 miles of cross-country skiing). On the weekends, families with kids ages 5 and up can also try the tubing park.

In March, Black Mountain is home to a Family Fun Weekend, with live music, sledding, s'mores by the fire pit, ski races, and more fun.

Eaton Mountain Ski Area & Snowtubing
89 Lambert Road
Skowhegan
(207) 474-2666
eatonmountain.com

Eaton Mountain is mainly a snowtubing park that offers evening tubing and a convenient lift uphill. There is also a section of the mountain, called the Lower Bowl, which is open to downhill skiing. Skiing is wonderfully affordable here, as kids 12 and under ski for free with a paying adult. Ski and snowboard rentals and a snack bar can be found in the modest base lodge. The mountain is open on weekends and school vacation weeks only.

Downeast and Northern

Big Squaw
447 Ski Resort Road
Greenville Junction
(207) 695-2400
skibigsquaw.com

Big Squaw is a community-run ski resort that is currently open Friday through Sunday and school vacation weeks. This mountain is best for hardy, intermediate-level skiers (there are 11 intermediate trails in all). What makes Big Squaw special is its sweeping views of Moosehead Lake. Meals are available in the lodge. The mountain is also home to 5 miles of groomed cross-country skiing and snow-shoe trails (donation only).

Mount Jefferson
Route 6
Lee
(207) 738-2377
skimtjefferson.com

This family-owned mountain, with its modest 430-foot vertical drop, is perfect for kids who are new to the sport. Families will also find a snowtubing park. There is a little red lodge where you can find ski and snowboarding rentals and homemade treats. Mount Jefferson is open for skiing and tubing on Saturdays, Sundays, and during school vacations.

Bigrock Ski Area
37 Graves Road
Mars Hill
(207) 425-6711
bigrockmaine.com

Located near Presque Isle, Bigrock Mountain is a dream for families. You'll enjoy affordable lift tickets and lessons plus thoughtful additions including a section of the mountain designated for families and a magic carpet for little ones. Bigrock also offers night skiing, a rail park, and a weekend tubing park with an 800-foot-long hill (kids must be 42 inches tall to ride). Warm up in the cozy base lodge, where you'll find a cafe. **Note:** The ski area is closed Mondays and Tuesdays with the exception of school vacation weeks.

Quoggy Jo Ski Center
420 Fort Road
Presque Isle
(207) 764-3248

At 215 vertical feet, this may be the smallest ski mountain in Maine, but the community-operated ski club offers the best value. The lift tickets and rental packages are priced low and kids can sign up for free ski and snowboard lessons.

WinterKids

If you're looking for special discounts for your family, consider the WinterKids app. This membership program gives kids the chance to try many of Maine's cross-country skiing and downhill ski areas, and other winter attractions, for free or at a discounted price.

The app, which is for kids ages 5-17, is designed for families of five or fewer, but WinterKids is also happy to accommodate larger families. too. It's a resource my family has enjoyed for years, and well worth the annual membership.

www.winterkids.org

The ski club also schedules fun events, from a ski sale during the first Sunday in November to a February vacation week celebration with a light parade, fireworks, night skiing, and more fun.

Lonesome Pine Trails

2 Forest Avenue
Fort Kent
(207) 834-5202
lonesomepines.org

The northernmost ski area in the state, Lonesome Pines is the finish line for the Can Am International Sled Dog Race, which is held every year in March (see page 37). The mountain, which is a convenient walking distance to downtown Fort Kent, is affordable and great for all levels of skiers. Lonesome Pine also supports **Maine Adaptive** (maineadaptive. org), a program for physically challenged kids and adults. Families will discover a snowpark for tricks, night skiing on Friday evenings, and Nordic trails operated by the **Fort Kent Outdoor Center** (see page 125). Lonesome Pine Trails is open on Wednesdays, Fridays, Saturdays, and Sundays with the exception of school vacation weeks.

Bigrock Ski Area, Mars Hill

Farm Visits, Markets+Sleigh Rides

During this time of year, when the holidays are top of mind, my family turns to local tree farms for our decorations. We've made it a family tradition to cut down our tree together, and despite a few debates about which tree is best, it's a favorite outing of ours. Similarly, we'll often visit indoor farmers' markets to find locally made gifts and treats for our holiday table.

As winter progresses, my family tries to make a bucket list of the new things we want to do. Those adventures have taken us on horse-drawn sleigh rides through the woods and dog sledding across snowy fields. It's our way of embracing a long winter and making the most of the season.

Southern

Chase Farms
1488 North Berwick Road
Wells
(207) 646-7888
chasefarmswells.com

Chase Farms might surprise you. While at first glance it seems like a busy roadside farmstand, the vast acreage behind that stand is something to experience. There is also a rustic barn that is home to Bob, Bill, Tom, and Jack—four Belgian horses that take families on scenic rides through the woods.

Holmes Tree Farm
193 Whitten Road
Kennebunk
(207) 985-3778
holmestreefarm.com

Named the #1 tree farm in the state by New England Christmas Tree Association, the historic Holmes Tree Farm is worth a trip. Santa visits on Saturdays and Sundays in a little red house, and families can enjoy warm cider donuts or hot dogs at lunch. Families can choose and cut their trees, or select a pre-cut tree. This farm accepts cash and check only (there is an ATM on site). Free hot cider is served in the gift shop.

Rockin' Horse Stable, Kennebunkport, Photo by Vanessa Thelin Photography

Rockin' Horse Stables

245 Arundel Road
Kennebunkport
(207) 967-4288
rockinhorsemaine.com

While going on a sleigh ride might cost more than some farm visits, the experience is worth it. At Rockin' Horse Stables, families board an authentic sleigh that is pulled by their impressive draft horses. The half-hour ride begins at their century-old barn, taking riders through farm fields surrounded by tall evergreens. After your sleigh ride, enjoy hot chocolate and a warm fire. Call ahead to reserve your seats.

The Old Farm Christmas Place

1148 Sawyer Road
Cape Elizabeth
(207) 799-0096
oldfarmchristmas.com

My family has enjoyed visiting The Old Farm Christmas Place for years, although we have learned that getting there early in the season is key to the best selection. While their balsam fir trees cost more than at some farms, the trees are pruned to perfection and last for weeks. Families can walk or take a wagon ride uphill to reach the fields of trees. You'll find some trees have already been selected by local families (marked by all nature of Santa Claus hats and stripy knit scarves). After choosing a tree, there's a fire pit nearby with marshmallows for roasting and a snack shack offering free cocoa and hot cider. The farm also has a cozy shop featuring locally made goods, music boxes, and other thoughtful gifts.

Hanscome's Christmas Tree Farm
194 Mountfort Road
North Yarmouth
(207) 831-2311

If you're searching for a quieter, cut-your-own-tree experience, Hanscome's Tree Farm is the place to go. When you arrive, you'll find a small shack decorated with wreaths and kissing balls. Select a saw and walk into the vast fields to choose your tree (most are balsam firs). There is one reasonable price for all trees, and the farm accepts cash only. You may want to bring boots or Wellies, as the grounds can be muddy if the temperatures are moderate.

Midcoast

Brunswick Winter Market
Fort Andross Mill, 14 Maine Street
Brunswick
brunswickwintermarket.net

When the weather isn't cooperating, there's no better place to spend a Saturday morning with kids than an indoor market. Grab breakfast, listen to live music, and talk with local vendors. It's amazing how much everyone can learn at a winter market, and this one, which boasts more than 50 vendors, is well worth a visit.

Balsam Hill Farm
Barrett Hill Road
Hope
(207) 975-4343

If you love a fragrant balsam fir tree that's naturally grown, this lovely hilltop farm is sure to become a favorite. Roam the fields with family and choose your own tree, or if you prefer less effort, simply select a pre-cut tree from the lot (the farm uses an honor system box when the lot isn't staffed). What's especially endearing about Balsam Hill Farm is its Unique and Unusual field, where you can find a sweet Charlie Brown tree to care for and call your own.

Christmas Tree Bazaar
174 Back Meadow Road
Nobleboro
(207) 563-5700
christmastreebazaar.com

Owner David Schaible has put his forestry background to good use with this lovely Christmas tree farm. Schaible has been harvesting balsam fir trees for more than 30 years and his attention to detail shows. After you choose your tree, visit the modest holiday shop for warm cocoa or hot coffee to reward your efforts. The Christmas Tree Bazaar also sells wreaths, garlands, and fresh greens.

Davis Stream Tree Farm
263 Hopkins Road
Washington
(207) 845-2544

This balsam fir tree farm is known for its stunning locale above Damariscotta Lake and meticulously groomed affordable trees. Local families return year after year to choose and cut the perfect tree to take home for the holidays. Dogs are welcome, too.

Lakes and Mountains

Ten Apple Farm
241 Yarmouth Road
Gray
(207) 657-7880
tenapplefarm.com

Ten Apple Farm is home to a sweet herd of Alpine dairy goats, and throughout the year owners Margaret Hathaway and Karl Schatz offer hour-long goat hikes in the 17-acre woods behind their property. My family visited during the winter and loved learning all about the goats— from their curious eating habits (white pine needles are a favorite) to their playful personalities. This 1.5 hike is best for kids ages 5 and up, but children under four can be carried. If you go, be sure to call ahead or get tickets online to make a reservation.

North Parish Christmas Tree Farm
231 North Parish Road
Turner
(207) 225-3382
npctfarm.com

The Rabon family has created a warm and welcoming tree farm. Visit to choose and cut your own balsam fir, and then stay to shop all of the beautiful

Heywood Kennel Sled Dog Adventures, Augusta

homemade gifts the family has made, including holiday lip balms in vanilla bean and peppermint flavors. You'll also find wreaths, kissing balls, and garlands to decorate your home.

Heywood Kennel Sled Dog Adventures
25 Church Hill Road
Augusta
(207) 629-9260

Partners Colby Briggs and Erin Noll offer the chance to try dogsledding with their friendly group of Alaskan Huskies. Two people at a time can sit in the sled while Colby and a team of six dogs take you on a half-hour ride through the open fields behind their home. After your ride, you're welcome to visit with

the dogs and enjoy a warm cocoa or coffee inside their warming hut.

Gooley's Christmas Tree Farm
263 Cowen Hill Road
Farmington
(207) 778-2368

What's especially sweet about Gooley's Farm is that the owners follow an Old German tradition of hiding pickle ornaments in the trees for children to find. There are ten pickles hidden each season, and each child who finds one wins a small prize. After selecting your tree, visit the warming yurt for mulled cider, hot cocoa, and cookies.

Winterberry Farm

538 Augusta Road (Route 27)
Belgrade
(207) 649-3331
winterberryfarmstand.com

In early December, this 40-acre organic farm hosts a two-day open house where families can visit for sleigh rides, gingerbread cookie decorating, and barn tours. Throughout the season, you can visit to choose one of their organic balsam trees and their team of oxen will haul it back to your car for you (just call ahead to let them know you're coming). If that weren't enough to entice you, the farm also has a lovely farmstand and cafe with homemade treats and handmade gifts. You can also visit for sleigh rides throughout the season—options range from a simple, 30-minute ride to a more elaborate and more expensive, 2-hour ride that includes a picnic lunch, hot tea, and a campfire.

Drafty Acres Farm

570 Main Street
Palmyra
(207) 416-8132

Owner Tyler Norris offers private rides for up to twelve people with his handsome team of horses on weekends (there is also a single-horse sleigh for two to three people). For a reasonable fee, your family can take a 30-minute ride through scenic woodland trails.

Downeast and Northern

Piper Mountain Christmas Tree Farm

27 Trundy Road
Newburgh
(207) 234-4300
pipermtn.com

This stunning tree farm, which was featured in *Martha Stewart Living Magazine* and *The Pioneer Woman*, offers an impressive variety of meticulously cared for trees. Families visit to choose and cut their trees and stay to peruse the festive gift shop, which also offers hot spiced cider, coffee, and donuts.

Nutkin Knoll Farm and Sugarworks

269 Chapman Road
Newburgh
(207) 234-7268
maine-christmas-trees.com

Nancy and Len Price make visitors feel right at home at their choose-and-cut farm, where families can select from Meyer spruce, Turkish, Korean, or balsam firs. After you select your tree, warm up with a cup of hot cider or shop the farm's beautiful selection of wreaths. Don't forget to take home some maple syrup, too.

Bangor's European Market
Sunnyside Greenhouse
117 Buck Street
Bangor
(207) 947-8464
sunnyside-greenhouses.com

This is a year-round, indoor market, but during Saturday mornings in the winter, it can also be a comforting haven from the cold. Kids can learn about world foods, all while enjoying everything from gorgeous local produce to tempting homemade donuts.

Orono Winter Market
Pine Street Parking Lot
Orono
(207) 323-8642

This is the rare winter market that is held outdoors, and remarkably, over two dozen farmers and artisans participate. A good attitude toward winter weather is a requirement, your family will be treated with good things like made-to-order crepes and locally roasted organic coffee. The market runs every Saturday in December and every second and fourth Saturday January through April.

Wild Iris Horse Farm, LLC
2 Lakewood Farm Road
Bar Harbor
(207) 288-5234
wildirishorsefarm.com

If you're fortunate enough to visit Bar Harbor during the quieter winter months, consider a private or public carriage ride with the farm's impressive team of English Shires. When the weather is just right, the storybook experience brings you down rural roads while sleigh bells jingle brightly. Families can sip hot cocoa as they snuggle under the warmth of a wool blanket. The farm offers both weekday and weekend rides for up to ten people.

Wild Iris Horse Farm, LLC, Bar Harbor

Winter ❄ Events

Yes, winter is long in Maine, but there's no shortage of unique events to discover. The festivities kick off before the holidays with local parades and fairs, and continue through February with all variety of winter carnivals. Even on the coldest of days, these community-powered festivals provide a great reason for families to spend a day out together.

Southern

Lighting of Nubble Lighthouse
11 Sohier Park Road
York
(207) 363-1040
nubblelight.org

This is a friend's favorite holiday event and while the seaside location can be bitingly cold, she says the lighting of this iconic lighthouse and its outbuildings is nothing short of magical. To beat the crowds, take the free shuttle bus from Ellis Park at Short Sands Beach (where there is generous parking). While you wait, enjoy carols from the York High School Chamber singers and a visit from Santa himself, plus hot cocoa and cookies.

Portland Tree Lighting
Monument Square
Portland
(207) 772-6828
portlandmaine.com

Downtown Portland is bright and beautiful during the holidays, and the tree lighting adds to its many charms. There's nothing like seeing a 40-foot tree come to life with 3,000 glowing lights, and little ones will also enjoy seeing Santa arrive. During the same weekend, free carriage rides are also available, beginning at Monument Square and taking you through the city, where you'll see whimsical lights by local artist Pandora LaCasse.

Chabad of Maine Menorah Parade
11 Pomeroy Street
Portland
(207) 871-8947
chabadofmaine.com

Celebrate Hanukkah with this bright and festive parade that begins at Chabad of Maine and ends at Portland City Hall (389 Congress Street). The Mayor of Portland shares a few words before the Grand Menorah Lighting. Families will especially enjoy live music, entertainment, warm latkes and donuts, chocolate gelt and dreidels.

Freeport Sparkle Celebration
Various locations, downtown Freeport
(207) 865-1212
visitfreeport.com

This town-wide event kicks off with a colorful, lighted holiday parade on Main Street. Throughout the weekend, you will find festive activities to experience, including horse-drawn carriage rides down Main Street, visits with the town's famous Talking Christmas Tree, and crafts, tastings, and activities at several local shops.

L.L.Bean is also a popular place to visit during the celebration, as visitors will discover a photo-ready campus aglow with hundreds of lighted trees. The Flagship location is also home to a live reindeer barn, where Santa and his team visits on weekends in December. Free admission.

Kennebunkport Christmas Prelude
Downtown Kennebunkport
(207) 967-0857
christmasprelude.com

This two-week event, which has been in existence for more than thirty years, begins soon after Thanksgiving; check the website for specific dates. Little ones will especially enjoy Santa's visit by lobster boat and the tree lighting in Dock Square. Families of all ages will want to experience the bonfire at the Fire Station and fireworks, plus a hat parade where everyone gets to show off their most festive holiday hats while marching along with a fife and drum duo.

Midcoast

Gardens Aglow
Coastal Maine Botanical Gardens
132 Botanical Gardens Drive
Boothbay
(207) 633-8000
mainegardens.org

This wildly popular, not-to-be-missed event is a festive holiday outing for families of all ages. When you arrive, you'll be met with a winter garden adorned with thousands of brightly colored lights. Walk wide paths over lighted bridges, through arbors, and around ponds. Along the way, you'll find warming fires and snacks to purchase. Kids can also take part in a scavenger hunt around the gardens.

In November and December, Boothbay celebrates the holidays with a **Festival of Lights**, (www.boothbayharbor.com), which is best known for its lighted boat parade on the harbor. The town-wide event also features visits from Santa and Mrs. Claus, horse-drawn carriage rides, caroling and a festival of trees.

If you and your family are planning a weekend visit to Boothbay, little ones will enjoy a ride on the **North Pole Express** at Boothbay Railway Village (railwayvillage.org/event/north-pole-express), which runs on Saturdays and Sundays through mid-December. Kids can meet Santa and enjoy hot cocoa and cookies, and go home with a keepsake ornament. **Note:** Be sure to order tickets in advance.

Winter Fest
Coastal Rivers' Salt Bay Farm & Nature Center
110 Belvedere Road
Damariscotta
(207) 563-1393
damariscottariver.org

This free annual event is a great way to enjoy a winter afternoon with your family. Visit for activities that include sledding, snowshoeing, crafts and games. There's also a campfire and marshmallows to roast, plus hot chocolate to enjoy. There are snowshoes on-hand for borrowing or bring your own. While you're there, take time to snowshoe or cross-country ski the trails of this lovely, 115-acre preserve with views of the Damariscotta River and Great Salt Bay.

Camden Winterfest
Townwide throughout Camden
(207) 236-4404
camdenmaineexperience.com

This weeklong celebration has something for everyone in the family. The festival

Coastal Maine Botanical Gardens, Boothbay

Camden Snow Bowl,
Camden

begins with a host of fun activities, including an ice sculpture contest and freestyle skiing competition in Harbor Park, crafts and stories for little ones at the library, and family entertainment at the beautiful Camden Opera House (camdenoperahouse.com). The week caps off with the US National Toboggan Championships, where teams with quirky names compete in costume, at the Camden Snow Bowl (see page 132) and a snow plow parade down Main Street.

Lakes and Mountains

Twin Cities Holiday Celebration
Downtown Lewiston and Auburn
(207) 513-3018
lewistonmaine.gov

For me, this big holiday celebration is reminiscent of the parade scene in *A Christmas Story*—the twin cities of Lewiston and Auburn come together to create a parade to remember. Watch as festive floats and community groups make their way through the city streets in Auburn to Lewiston. The parade ends with a lighting of the city tree and menorah, free hot chocolate and treats, wagon rides, and photos with Mr. and Mrs. Claus.

Keeping Christmas
Washburn Norlands Living History Center
290 Norlands Road
Livermore
(207) 897-4366
norlands.org

Israel and Martha Washburn raised ten children at Norlands during the 19th century. Seven of those children grew up to become a governor, a congressman, a United States senator, Secretary of State, foreign minister, a Civil War general, and a Navy captain. Today, their ancestral home is open to visitors. A holiday visit to Norlands is a memorable experience. Families can tour the mansion and learn about what life was like in the 19th century. Kids can string popcorn for the tree, make 19th-century crafts, listen to stories, and attend class in a one-room schoolhouse. Homemade treats including cookies, hot mulled cider, and soups are served to guests. If weather cooperates, wagon rides are offered on the grounds.

Chester Greenwood Day
Townwide
Farmington
(207) 778-4215
franklincountymaine.org

This quirky community event celebrates

the founder of earmuffs, one Mr. Chester Greenwood, who hailed from Farmington. Visit Main Street for an irresistible earmuff-themed parade. While the parade is a highlight, the town also has gingerbread houses on display and more special events, including the Taste of Farmington, where families can sample foods from local restaurants. You can also watch a brave few from the Polar Bear Club jump in Clearwater Lake, a popular ice fishing spot with views of Bannock Mountain.

World's Greatest Sleigh Ride
400 Main Street
Lisbon Falls

Run by the Pejepscot Sno-Chiefs Snowmobile Club, this event raises money for a different Maine-based non-profit organization each year. For a reasonable rate, you can take a sleigh ride through fields and woods. After your ride, a mobile snack shack serves up warm drinks, stew, and homemade donuts.

Maine Lakes Winter Carnival
Townwide throughout Bridgton
(207) 647-3472
mainelakeschamber.com

If you are itching to get outside for a few hours with your kids, this February

festival will certainly keep the whole family entertained. Children can take part in a kids' fishing derby (registration required for kids 16 and under). Watch a magic show, see brave Mainers take a polar plunge in the lake to benefit a local animal shelter, or go to a fireworks show at night.

Downeast and Northern

Festival of Lights Parade
Downtown Bangor
bangorrotary.org

The Rotary Club of Bangor knows how to put together a great parade, as evidenced by the thousands of onlookers that show up each year. This parade has more than 70 floats, marching bands, dancers and local clubs celebrating Hanukkah, Christmas, Kwanzaa, and the solstice. During the event, Santa visits downtown for holiday cookie decorating, and a city tree lighting happens in West Market Square.

Ellsworth Winter Carnival
Various locations in Ellsworth
(207) 667-2563
ellsworthmaine.gov

There is so much fun to be had at this community-inspired carnival. The

Woodlawn Museum (woodlawnmuseum.com), a restored 19th-entury estate with expansive grounds, has cardboard sled races for all ages. The local snowmobile club also offers free rides around the property. At nearby **Knowlton Park** (11 Shore Road), families can enjoy, public skating. The carnival concludes with an impressive fireworks show at Ellsworth High School (299 State Street). All events are free.

Family Fun Day
Aroostook State Park
87 State Park Road
Presque Isle
(207) 768-8341
maine.gov/aroostook

This is a day that's sure to delight kids of all ages. A ski and snowshoe trailer is at the park so families new to these sports can give them a try. If the weather cooperates, you'll also have the opportunity to sled on park hills or skate on Echo Lake. The fee to take part is remarkably reasonable and it's free for kids 12 and under.

Calendar  of Events

Here, you'll find a helpful list of fairs, festivals, and special events mentioned throughout this book. For planning purposes, the events are listed by month. If you're considering going to a fair or festival with family, be sure to check the event website or Facebook page ahead of time, as dates are often subject to change. Some fairs and festivals occur during the same week or weekend year after year. You'll find those noted below.

FEBRUARY

Camden Winterfest, Camden, 152

Ellsworth Winter Carnival, Ellsworth, 157

Family Fun Day, Mount Blue State Park, Weld, 129

Family Fun Day, Aroostook State Park, Presque Isle, 157

Maine Lakes Winter Carnival, Bridgton, 156

US National Toboggan Championships, Camden, 155

Winter Fest, Damariscotta, 152

World's Greatest Sleigh Ride, Lisbon Falls, 156

MARCH

Cam-Am International Crown Sled Dog Races, Fort Kent, 37

Family Fun Weekend, Black Mountain, Rumford, 138

Maine Maple Sunday, statewide (fourth Sunday in March), 25-26, 29-31

Moose Dash, Rangeley, 36

St. Patrick's Day Parade, Portland, 32

Young at Art, Hallowell, 36

APRIL

Copper Tail Farm Kid Hugging Day, Waldoboro, 35

Portland Sea Dogs Opening Day, Portland, 33

MAY

Aldermere Farm Calf Unveiling Day, Rockport, 35

Alewife Festival, Damariscotta Mills, 35-36

Bug Light Kite Festival, South Portland, 33

Coastal Maine Botanical Gardens Opening Day, Boothbay, 35

Eden Farmers Market Opens, Bar Harbor, 37

Huttopia Maine Opening Day, Sanford, 32-33

Kid Central Festival, Bangor, 38

Maine Fiddlehead Festival, Farmington, 36

McLaughlin Garden Lilac Festival, South Paris, 37

Skyline Farm Plow Day, North Yarmouth, 33

JUNE

Cape Farm Alliance Strawberry Fest, Cape Elizabeth (fourth weekend of June), 78

New Gloucester Strawberry Festival, New Gloucester, 80

Peony Festival, Maine Audubon's Gilsland Farm, Falmouth, 78

South Berwick Strawberry Festival, South Berwick, 78

The Maine Whoopie Pie Festival, Dover-Foxcroft, 82

Windjammer Days, Boothbay Harbor (fourth Saturday in June), 79

JULY

Bath Heritage Days, Bath (July 4th weekend), 80

Harbor House Flamingo Festival, Southwest Harbor, 82

Maine Open Farms Day, statewide, 72

Maine Potato Blossom Festival, Fort Fairfield (third Saturday in July), 83

Ossipee Valley Music Festival, South Hiram, 82

Painted Lady Butterfly Release, Charlotte Rhoades Garden, Southwest Harbor, 71

Yarmouth Clam Festival, Yarmouth (starts the third Friday in July), 79

AUGUST

Great Falls Balloon Festival, Lewiston, 82

Maine Lobster Festival, Rockland (first weekend of August), 80

Ploye Festival and International Muskie Derby, Fort Kent, 83

Union Fair and Maine Wild Blueberry Festival, Union, 80

SEPTEMBER

Acadia Night Sky Festival, Mount Desert Island, 115

Apple Acres Farm Bluegrass Festival, Hiram, 110

Bethel Harvest Festival, Bethel, 112

Blue Hill Fair, Blue Hill, 113

Capriccio: Festival of Kites, Ogunquit (Labor Day weekend), 105

Common Ground Country Fair, Unity (third weekend after Labor Day), 110

Cumberland Fair, Cumberland, 106

Eastport Pirate Festival, Eastport, 113

Machias Bay Harvest Fair, Machias, 113

Maine Apple Sunday, statewide, 98

Maine Apple Day Celebration, Falmouth, 106

Maine Open Lighthouse Day, statewide, 105

Pineland Farms Harvest Festival, New Gloucester, 110

Scarecrow Festival, Fort Kent, 115

OCTOBER

Camp Sunshine Pumpkin Festival, Freeport, 106

Damariscotta Pumpkinfest & Regatta, Damariscotta (Columbus Day weekend), 109

Fall Foliage Festival, Boothbay (Columbus Day weekend), 108

Fryeburg Fair, Fryeburg, 112

Maine Craft Weekend, statewide, 105

Night Maze Event, Treworgy Orchard, Levant, 103

Nobleboro Applefest, Nobleboro, 109

Pettengill Farm Day, Freeport, 89

Shawnee Peak Fall Festival, Bridgton, 110

The Pumpkin Event, Spring Brook Farm, Cumberland, 106

NOVEMBER

Festival of Lights, Boothbay, 152

Gardens Aglow, Boothbay, 152

Lighting of Nubble Lighthouse, York, 150

Portland Tree Lighting, Monument Square, Portland (day after Thanksgiving), 150

Rolling Slumber Bed Races, Brunswick, 108

Twin Cities Holiday Celebration, Lewiston and Auburn, 155

DECEMBER

Chabad of Maine Menorah Parade , 151

Chester Greenwood Day, Farmington, 156

Festival of Lights Parade, Bangor (first Saturday of December), 156

Freeport Sparkle Celebration, Freeport, 151

Kennebunkport Christmas Prelude, Kennebunkport, 151

Keeping Christmas, Livermore, 155

North Pole Express, Boothbay, 152

U-Pick Crops: What's in Season When

You'll find suggestions for what to pick each season throughout the book, but this at-a-glance list lets you know what is available June through December. If you're visiting a farm, always check their website or Facebook page for hours, availability, and up-to-date picking information.

JUNE
Strawberries

JULY
Blackberries
Highbush blueberries
Raspberries
Strawberries

AUGUST
Apples
Highbush blueberries
Peaches
Raspberries
Wild blueberries

SEPTEMBER
Apples
Fall raspberries
Highbush blueberries
Peaches
Pumpkins

OCTOBER
Apples
Cranberries
Highbush blueberries
Peaches
Pumpkins

NOVEMBER
Cranberries
Christmas trees

DECEMBER
Christmas trees

Where  to Swim
at a Glance

Whether you're visiting Maine or have summer guests in town, it's helpful to have a quick list of swimming spots at the ready. Below, you'll find all the suggestions mentioned in the book with call-outs for freshwater and saltwater options.

The tides can be tricky in Maine (high tide can leave you with less beach to enjoy), so be sure to check a tide chart app before you go to any saltwater beaches.

FRESHWATER SWIMMING

Midcoast
Barrett's Cove Public Beach, Camden, 53, 175
Damariscotta Lake State Park, Jefferson, 55

Lakes and Mountains
Bresca and the Honey Bee at Outlet Beach, New Gloucester, 57
Cathedral Pines Campground, Eustis, 59
Highland Lake Beach, Bridgton, 58, 176
Moy-Mo-Day-O Recreation Area, Limington, 57
Mount Blue State Park, Weld, 58
Range Pond State Park, Poland, 58
Sebago Lake State Park, Casco, 58, 176
Webb Lake, Weld, 176

Downeast and Northern Points
Echo Lake Beach, Southwest Harbor, 178

Jones Pond, Gouldsboro, 60
Lily Bay State Park, Beaver Cove, 59
Peaks-Kenny State Park, Dover-Foxcroft, 60
Portage Lake Public Beach, Portage Lake, 61
Simpson Pond, Roque Bluffs State Park, Roque Bluffs, 61

SALTWATER SWIMMING

Southern
Crescent Beach State Park, Cape Elizabeth, 49, 174
Drakes Island Beach, Wells, 51
Ferry Beach State Park, Saco, 52
Footbridge Beach, Ogunquit, 51
Goose Rocks Beach, Kennebunkport, 51
Kettle Cove State Park, Cape Elizabeth, 49, 174
Long and Short Sands Beaches, York Beach, 50

Echo Lake Beach, Southwest Harbor

Explore Outdoors

While you'll find suggestions for hikes and outdoor exploration by season throughout this book, many of the parks and preserves mentioned can be enjoyed all through the year. Following is a complete list of places to explore by region with notes for when it is best to visit.

SOUTHERN

Androscoggin River Bicycle Path, Brunswick and Topsham
Photo by Anna Jordan

Sebago to the Sea Trail, Standish, Gorham and Windham (spring, summer, fall), 20

Pineland Farms, New Gloucester (year-round), 110, 122

Pleasant Mountain, Bridgton (year-round), 66, 176

Quarry Road Trails, Waterville (year-round), 124, 184

Rattlesnake Mountain, Raymond (summer, fall), 93

Roberts Farm Preserve, Norway (year-round), 123

Sabattus Mountain, Lovell (year-round), 66

Sawyer Mountain, Limerick (spring, summer, fall), 101

Shepard's Farm Preserve, Norway (year-round), 92

Spring Road Trail, Auburn (year-round), 102

Step Falls, Newry (summer, fall), 95

Vaughan Woods, Hallowell (year-round), 173

DOWNEAST AND NORTHERN

Acadia Carriage Road Trails, Acadia National Park (year-round), 124

Acadia National Park Park Loop, Bar Harbor (summer, fall), 71

Aroostook State Park, Presque Isle (year-round), 96

Bangor City Forest, Bangor (year-round), 22

Bar Harbor Shore Path, Bar Harbor (spring, summer, fall), 22

Bass Harbor Head Light, Tremont (summer, fall), 22, 173

Caribou Ski Center, Caribou (winter), 125

Charlotte Rhoades Park, Southwest Harbor (spring, summer, fall), 71

Crockett Cove Woods, Deer Isle (summer, fall), 69

Debsconeag Ice Caves, Debsconeag Wilderness Area (summer, fall), 69

Fort Kent Outdoor Center, Fort Kent (year-round), 125, 140

Gorham Mountain Trail, Bar Harbor (summer, fall), 96

Holbrook Island Sanctuary, Brookville (year-round), 124

Jasper Beach Park, Machiasport (spring, summer, fall), 96

Lamoine State Park, Lamoine (spring, summer, fall), 60, 95, 180

Little Abol Falls, Millinocket (summer, fall), 97

Moxie Falls, The Forks (spring, summer, fall), 69, 176

Nordic Heritage Center, Presque Isle (year-round), 22, 125

Orono Bog Boardwalk, Bangor (spring, summer, fall), 22

Wonderland Trail, Southwest Harbor (spring, summer, fall), 22, 173

Recommended Day Trips

When I'm planning a day trip for my husband and children, I try to find a few interesting places within a reasonable radius (30 minutes or less from one destination to the next is doable for my crew). I also keep more active visits to the morning, and quieter exploration for the afternoon, as my kids tend to have more energy earlier in the day. Mine is also a family of food lovers, so I'll seek out restaurants, markets, and cafes for a treat or a meal. With this criteria in mind, following are some tried-and-true day trips for your family to enjoy:

SPRING
SOUTHERN
Trip 1: Kennebunkport/Kennebunk
Spend the morning walking the trails at **Smith Preserve** (76 Guinea Road) in Kennebunkport or explore the **Seashore Trolley Museum** (195 Log Cabin Road), which opens to visitors in May. Bring a picnic lunch and experience what it's like to ride in an old-fashioned trolley car. **Snug Harbor Farm** (87 Western Avenue) in nearby Kennebunk is a fun place for kids and adults to visit. Young children will enjoy seeing the miniature horses, chickens, peacocks, and pheasants. Adults will appreciate the ornamental plants and thoughtfully curated garden shop.

Trip 2: South Portland
Visit two unique lighthouses—the diminutive **Bug Light** (Bug Light Park, Madison Street), which is known for its Greek-inspired design and **Spring Point Ledge Lighthouse** (Fort Road, Southern Maine Community College), where you can explore the breakwater that leads to it, as well as **Old Fort Preble** (Bunker Lane, Southern Maine Community College), a 19th-century military fort. All three locations have sweeping views of Portland Harbor and the Casco Bay Islands. If you're searching for a quick breakfast or lunch, nearby **Scratch Baking Co.** (416 Preble Street) is a popular spot for bagels, but their pastries and sandwiches are also excellent.

Trip 3: Portland
If the weather isn't cooperating, start the morning with brunch at **Rí Rá** (72 Commercial Street), where you'll find views of the working waterfront from the second-floor dining room. For younger children, the **Children's Museum and Theatre of Maine**

(kitetails.org) offers an imaginative indoor play space, special events, and plays performed by local children.

Trip 4: Yarmouth/Cumberland

A walk in Yarmouth's **Royal River Park** (111 East Elm Street) is a great way to start the day. Families can explore the trails near to the river, play in the fields, or enjoy a picnic together. After your walk, drive country roads to **Sunflower Farm Creamery** (12 Harmon Way) in Cumberland. Visit their sweet baby goats and farm animals or take home some creamy goat milk cheeses from the self-serve fridge.

MIDCOAST

Trip 1: Camden/Rockland area

Merryspring Nature Center (30 Conway Road) in Camden is a lovely place to visit any time of year. Families can explore the woodland trails or simply enjoy the open space. After spending the morning outside, little ones might like to play at the **Coastal Children's Museum** (75 Mechanic Street) in Rockland. Designed for children ages 2 through 9, the museum offers interactive exhibits and space for imaginative play. For older children, the **Owls Head Transportation Museum** (117 Museum Street, Owls Head) has vintage automobiles and planes on display. The museum

hosts family-friendly events throughout the year, so be sure to check their event listings before you go.

Trip 2: Boothbay

Get to know the beauty of Boothbay by walking **Ocean Point** (Shore Road), where you can scale rocks and explore coves. After your walk, visit the **Coastal Maine Botanical Gardens** (132 Botanical Gardens Drive) to see colorful spring blooms or play throughout the dreamy Children's Garden. The gardens are also home to a sunny cafe, where you'll find wholesome soups, salads, and sandwiches plus a menu for little ones.

LAKES AND MOUNTAINS

Trip 1: Sabattus/Gray

If you're traveling on the weekend, **Jillson's Farm & Sugarhouse** (143 Jordan Bridge Road) in Sabattus serves a hearty farm breakfast. Families can choose from scrambled eggs, pancakes, or French toast (you'll definitely want to try their maple syrup), pastries, baked beans, and sausage. If you visit in March or April, you can tour the sugarhouse and barn, where kids can meet the animals. After your visit, head to **Maine Wildlife Park** (56 Game Farm Road/Route 26) in Gray. The park, which opens in early May, is the place to learn about local wildlife from black bears to gangly moose.

Trip 2: Augusta/Hallowell

For families who enjoy exploring by bike, try the **Kennebec River Rail Trail** in Augusta (MSHA Parking Lot) and follow the paved path for 30 minutes (4.6 miles) to 2nd Street, which connects to the Vaughan Woods trailhead on Litchfield Road in Hallowell. While you cannot ride bikes on the woodland paths, it's an enchanting place for kids to take a break and explore historic stone bridges, streams, and waterfalls.

DOWNEAST AND NORTHERN
Trip 1: Bar Harbor

If it's your first time to Bar Harbor, the **Shore Path** (Ells Pier) is a great way to get to know the popular coastal town. Your family will enjoy seaside views, see historic homes, and learn a little bit about the town's history along the way. After your walk, visit the **Dorr Museum** (105 Eden Street), a natural history museum that is located at the College of the Atlantic. Kids can learn about local wildlife, visit a tide pool tank, or see the latest student exhibits. The museum is open Tuesday through Saturday.

Trip 2: Southwest Harbor/Tremont

A visit to the **Wonderland Trail** in Southwest Harbor (Seawall Road/102A) is a peaceful way to start the day with family. The 1.4-mile round-trip walk combines woodland paths and coastal views. After your walk, explore the rocky shore around 19th-century **Bass Harbor Head Light** (Lighthouse Road) in Tremont. If you're in the mood for generously sized lobster rolls and hand-cut fries, treat the family to lunch at **Beal's Lobster Pier** (182 Clark Point Road) back in Southwest Harbor. The menu also features vegetarian, gluten-free, and kid-friendly options. Beal's opens in May.

SUMMER
SOUTHERN POINTS
Trip 1: Wells

During June and July, **Spiller Farm** (85 Spiller Farm Lane) is the place to pick strawberries and raspberries in the early mornings. When you're done picking, stop at the farm store to purchase picnic provisions and drive 30 minutes to the **Rachel Carson National Wildlife Refuge** (321 Port Road), where you'll find a shaded picnic area and a scenic, 1-mile loop trail to traverse.

Trip 2: Scarborough

A morning paddle at the **Scarborough Marsh Audubon Center** (136 Pine Point Road) is a delight for all ages. Families can rent canoes or kayaks and explore the Dunstan River for up to two hours. After paddling, cool off at nearby **Pine Point Beach**, where you'll find

ample parking (a fee is charged between 9 a.m. to 5 p.m.), restrooms, and a concessions stand, should you need a bite to eat.

Trip 3: Cape Elizabeth

There is no shortage of breathtaking spaces to visit in Cape Elizabeth. For swimming, choose from peaceful **Kettle Cove State Park** (Ocean House Road) or if there are no parking spots available, take the short drive to **Crescent Beach State Park** (66 Bowery Beach Road) and enjoy the wide, sandy expanse of beach. Later in the day, pick up sandwiches at **C Salt Gourmet** (349 Ocean House Road) and bring them to **Two Lights State Park** (7 Tower Drive),

where you can picnic and enjoy dramatic ocean views. Kids will also have fun scaling the rocks along the water.

MIDCOAST

Trip 1: Harpswell

Take the family to explore the **Giant's Stairs** (19 Ocean Street, Bailey Island), which are named for the impressive volcanic rock that's eroded over time, appearing like steps that lead to the ocean. Your family can stick to the 0.3-mile loop or go off-trail and climb the rocky shoreline (keep a careful eye on your kids and wear sturdy shoes). After your visit, take a scenic drive to **Mitchell Field** (1410 Harpswell Neck Road/Route

Scarborough Marsh, Scarborough

123). Once a US Navy property, the 120-acre park offers a sandy beach and a quiet place to swim.

Trip 2: Rockport/Camden

Go for an early morning walk at **Beech Hill Preserve** in Rockport (Beech Hill Road), where a 0.6-mile one-way path leads to sweeping views of Penobscot Bay and Camden Hills. At the top of the hill, you'll find a 1917 stone hut known for its distinctive sod roof and slate patio. Or, if you have younger children, drive to **Aldemere Farm** (20 Russell Avenue), a bucolic location that's beloved for its award-winning Belted Galloways. The black-and-white-striped cows are the oldest operating herd in the United States. Make your way to Camden next for swimming at **Barrett's Cove Public Beach** (Beaucaire Avenue, off Route 52). The freshwater cove on Megunticook Lake is a beautiful place to cool off after a busy morning.

LAKES AND MOUNTAINS
Trip 1: Bridgton

At 1,600 feet elevation, climbing **Pleasant Mountain** (Route 302, past Shawnee Peak) requires some serious effort, but the 360-degree views of Moose Pond and the White Mountains makes the 1.8-mile (one-way) Ledges Trail hike worthwhile. Plus, you can look forward to swimming at **Highland Lake Beach** (Highland Road) after your climb. The grassy beach with mountain views is in convenient walking distance to town and has picnic tables if you want to pick up sandwiches at **Beth's Kitchen Cafe** (108 Main Street).

Trip 2: Weld

Spend the day at **Mount Blue State Park** (299 Center Hill Road) in Weld. Begin with a visit to the **Center Hill Nature Trail**, where kids can learn about the unique trees, leaves, and woodland creatures along the half-mile loop. If you bring snacks along, the picnic tables are a perfect place to pause and enjoy the view of Tumbledown and Jackson Mountains. After your walk, swim or rent boats to take out on **Webb Lake**.

Trip 3: Sebago/Casco

Bring along a cooler and start your day with a visit to **Crabtree's Blueberries** in Sebago (703 Bridgton Road). Fill tin pails with easy-to-pick highbush blueberries. Varieties and availability depend on the month so call ahead before you go (highbush blueberries are generally in season July through October). After a morning of blueberry picking, head to **Sebago Lake State Park** in Casco (11 Park Access Road) where you'll find a sparkling lake for swimming, a sandy beach, and a picnic area shaded by tall pines. There are charcoal grills next to the picnic tables, if you're planning a cookout with the family.

DOWNEAST AND NORTHERN
Trip 1: The Forks

If your kids are 8 and up, consider a weekend trip to **The Forks**, a popular destination for rafting on the Kennebec River. **The Northern Outdoors** (1771 US Route 201) offers cabins, campsites, and cabin-inspired condos. Plan on a morning hike to **Moxie Falls** (Lake Moxie Road) where a short, flat 1.2-mile round-trip walk will take you to the impressive 90-foot falls. After your hike, visit **The Northern Outdoors' Kennebec River Pub** for a hearty lunch and then head out on the river for a self-guided afternoon float trip with the kids.

Trip 2: Sedgwick/Deer Isle/ Stonington

In July and August, when wild blueberries are prevalent on the Maine coast, take the family to **Cooper Farm** at Caterpillar Hill (Cooper Farm Road, just after scenic turnout) in Sedgwick. The view alone makes the trip worthwhile, but the unique experience of foraging for wild blueberries is equally special. Bring your own buckets and be sure to wear long pants and plenty of bug spray to protect yourself from ticks. If you've

Center Hill Nature Trail, Weld

worked up an appetite, bring the kids to **El El Frijoles** (41 Caterpillar Hill Road) in nearby Sargentville, where you'll find fresh Mexican food and an inviting outdoor eating space (little ones will love the play area). After lunch, take a scenic drive over the Deer Isle Bridge into the coastal town of Stonington, where you'll spot lobster boats in the harbor and pretty coves for swimming. Plan an afternoon hike at the **Crockett Cove Woods Preserve** (Fire Road 88), a lush coastal forest where kids of any age will enjoy walking the shaded woodland trails.

Trip 3: Southwest Harbor
Start your morning with light and airy popovers at **The Common Good Cafe** (19 Clark Point Road) in the little town of Southwest Harbor. The community-run cafe also serves juice, coffee and oatmeal. Proceeds help fund their soup kitchen throughout the winter months. After breakfast, stop by **Charlotte Rhoades Park** (191 Main Street/Route 102) to stroll among the colorful perennials, where butterflies flutter about. Little kids will love running and playing on the lush green lawn that overlooks Norwood Cove. Then take the family for a day of swimming at **Echo Lake Beach** (Echo Lake Beach Road). You'll find convenient parking, changing rooms, and a sandy beach that overlooks

a vast lake with views of mountain cliffs.

FALL
SOUTHERN
Trip 1: York/Kittery
The beauty of **Mount Agamenticus** (Big A Universal Access Trail, Mountain Road) in York is that families of all ages can experience what it's like to be on top of a big mountain without the big climb. Drive to the top and then walk the 1-mile Big A Universal Access Trail loop, and on a clear day, you'll be treated to views of the Atlantic Ocean and White Mountains. After your visit to the mountain, drive to **Zach's Corn Maze** (7 Colby Road), where you can enjoy a hayride, explore the 12-acre maze or pick pumpkins in the fields. If the kids are hungry after so much activity, take them to **When Pigs Fly Pizzeria** (460 US Route One) in Kittery for wood-fired pizzas, hearty sandwiches and salads.

Trip 2: Pownal/North Yarmouth
Nothing beats a morning hike at **Bradbury Mountain State Park** (528 Hallowell Road) in Pownal. Walk the mile-long Northern Loop and, during peak season, you'll see an array of colors from its 484-foot peak. After your hike, drive rolling rural roads to **Hansel's Orchard** (44 Sweetser Road) in North Yarmouth.

Grab a basket and fill it to the brim with apples from this peaceful orchard.

MIDCOAST
Trip 1: Lincolnville
Fernald's Neck Preserve (Fernald's Neck Road) is a quiet place to explore. Walk among tall pines to Balance Rock, a large boulder which looks as if it's about to roll over on its side. You'll also enjoy views of Megunticook Lake and surrounding cliffs. After your walk, visit **Sewall Organic Orchard** (259 Masalin Road). The picturesque orchard, which is the oldest certified organic apple orchard in the state, sells apples, freshly pressed apple cider, and apple cider vinegar.

Trip 2: Belfast/Searsport/Prospect
Start your day at **Belfast Co-Op** (123 High Street), a natural food store and cafe, for baked goods and coffee, or pick up picnic provisions for later in the afternoon (I especially enjoy their impressive selection of Maine-made goods). Next, drive to **Moose Point State Park** (310 West Main Street) in Searsport where you can walk a 1.2-mile park loop path with views of the Penobscot Bay. If your family is ready for more exploration, continue to **Penobscot Narrows Bridge** and **Fort Knox** (Route 174, off US Route 1) in Prospect. The

19th-century granite fort is the ideal location for imaginative play. Kids can see barracks, storehouses, and cannons or explore among the fort's long passageways. Take a picnic break or visit the bridge and observatory. An elevator inside the observatory will take you up 42 stories, where you'll be treated to colorful autumn views along the Penobscot River.

LAKES AND MOUNTAINS
Trip 1: Rangeley/Byron/Peru
Bald Mountain (Bald Mountain Road) in Oquossoc requires only a mile-long hike to the summit. At the top, kids will have fun climbing the lookout platform, which offers views of Rangeley Lakes and the surrounding mountains. After your hike, drive scenic mountain roads to **Coos Canyon** (Route 17), where the Swift River created this stunning natural gorge. If the water is low, kids can spend time climbing on the rocks. Continue your trip to **Heritage Farm** (1062 Auburn Road) in Peru where you'll find an array of big, beautiful pumpkins.

Trip 2: Auburn/Turner
Wallingford's Fruit House (1240 Perkins Ridge Road) in Auburn is beloved by local families for cider donuts hot off the conveyor and homemade apple dumplings. Families also enjoy picking apples in the bountiful orchards. After

your visit, walk off all of those treats at **Androscoggin Riverlands State Park** (Center Bridge Road, off Route 4) in Turner. The 1.1-mile out-and-back Homestead Trail is a fun place to explore. You'll find the ruins of an old farmhouse and a path that leads to a picnic meadow with stunning views of the Androscoggin River.

DOWNEAST AND NORTHERN
Trip 1: Trenton/Ellsworth/Lamoine
On October weekends, families can pick organic cranberries in the bog at **Snugglemagic Farm** (1554 Bayside Road) in Trenton. Kids will also enjoy visiting with the sweet alpacas and goats. Next drive to Ellsworth's historic Main Street for lunch at **Flexit Cafe & Bakery** (192 Main Street). The sunny cafe has a selection of soups, salads, and sandwiches made with fresh, local ingredients. After lunch, drive to **Lamoine State Park** (23 State Park Road) for a relaxing, mile-long loop walk on the shores of Frenchman's Bay. Little ones will especially enjoy playing in the treehouse on the path.

Trip 2: Presque Isle/Caribou
Aroostook State Park (off US Route 1, south of Presque Isle) offers a steep climb up Quoggy Jo Mountain. While the hike to the North Peak is only 2.25 miles round-trip, it is best for kids 9 and up. If you have little ones, you can explore the shores of **Echo Lake**, picnic or play in the shaded playground area. Next drive to **Goughan Farms** (375 Fort Fairfield Road) in Caribou, where you'll find inspired homemade ice cream flavors like lemon basil and strawberry rhubarb. In the fall, families can also visit the challenging corn maze, which features a new design each year.

WINTER
SOUTHERN
Trip 1: Wells
Start with a fun morning outdoors at **Wells Reserve at Laudholm** (324 Laudholm Farm Road). Bring your own gear for skiing or snowshoeing the woodland and shoreline trails. Sledding at the hill near the historic farmhouse also makes for a memorable experience. After exploring, bring the family to **Chase Farms** (1488 North Berwick Road), where you can take a sleigh ride through the woods led by their team of Belgian horses. The farm store carries fresh baked goods and warm drinks in case you need a pick-me-up after the ride.

Trip 2: Kennebunk
The sweet town of Kennebunk has a covered outdoor ice skating rink all its own. Bring your own skates to the **Waterhouse Center** (51 Main Street) and glide on the ice to your heart's con-

tent. If you're looking for something to eat or drink, walk over to the **Boulangerie** bakery (5 Nasons Court) for incredible pastries, quiche, and pre-made sandwiches on their homemade breads. Next, travel just a few miles outside of town to **Holmes Tree Farm** (193 Whitten Road). Santa himself visits the farm on the weekends. You can also choose and cut your own balsam fir tree or select one that is already cut for you.

Trip 3: Yarmouth/North Yarmouth

The **Orland H. Blake Skating Pond** (188 Main Street) in Yarmouth is a lovely place to take the family ice skating. All you need is a thermos of hot cocoa or cider and your own skates. There is a warming hut at the pond with a cozy, open fire and benches. For a fun pre-holiday trip, follow up with a visit to **Hanscome's Christmas Tree Farm** (194 Mountfort Road) in North Yarmouth, where you can choose and cut your own balsam fir tree. Just be sure to bring cash along with you, as the farm does not accept checks or credit cards.

Hanscome's Christmas Tree Farm
North Yarmouth

Orland H. Blake Skating Pond, Yarmouth

MIDCOAST
Trip 1: Brunswick/Topsham
Begin your day with some shopping at the **Brunswick Winter Market** (Fort Andross Mill, 14 Maine Street), which has more than 50 local vendors to choose from, offering everything from freshly roasted coffee beans to farm-raised meats and handmade pottery. There are tables and chairs by the mill's lofty windows, should you want to sit and enjoy breakfast. Stay in town after your visit for outdoor skating at the **Brunswick Mall Ice Rink** (Lower Mall Park, Maine Street).

Trip 2: Damariscotta/Nobleboro
Round Top Farm (3 Round Top Lane) in Damariscotta is unique place to skate, as the preserve is home to a Victorian-era farmhouse and historic barn. Bring your own skates and enjoy the comfort of the warming hut, where hot cocoa is served on weekends. If you're visiting the area during the holidays, travel to **Christmas Tree Bazaar** (174 Back Meadow Road) in Nobleboro for a fragrant balsam fir tree. You'll also find a small shop with natural holiday décor and cocoa for the kids.

LAKES AND MOUNTAINS
Trip 1: Skowhegan/Palmyra
Enjoy a day of snowy adventures, begin-ning with tubing at **Eaton Mountain** (89 Lambert Road) in Skowhegan. If kids prefer, they can also ski or snow-board at the Lower Bowl of the moun-tain. If you go, just keep in mind that Eaton Mountain is open on weekends and school vacations only. When the kids are ready to slow down, consider a drive to **Drafty Acres Farm** (570 Main Street) in Palmyra. The farm offers half-hour private sleigh rides through the woods.

Trip 2: Belgrade/Waterville
There is nothing better than a win-try weekend morning trip to a farm. **Winterberry Farm** (538 Augusta Road) in Belgrade is a lovely place to visit, whether you're searching for an organic balsam tree or wanting to see the grounds by horse-drawn sleigh (the farm provides options for everything from a half-hour to a two-hour ride). If the weather cooperates, spend the second half of the day exploring at **Quarry Road Trails** (300 Quarry Road) in Waterville. For cross-country skiers the expansive park offers 6 miles of groomed trails. You can rent skis at the Welcome Center or try snowshoes, which are free of charge.

Trip 3: Auburn/Turner
Lost Valley (200 Lost Valley Road) in

Auburn is the answer for a family who enjoys a little bit of everything. Visit for snowboarding, downhill skiing, or Nordic skiing. On weekends, the snow-tubing park is also open. If it's close to the holidays, consider a visit to **North Parish Christmas Tree Farm** (231 North Parish Road) in Turner, to search for the perfect tree.

DOWNEAST AND NORTHERN
Trip 1: Newburgh/Bangor
If you're on the hunt for the perfect tree, there are two unique farms to choose from in Newburgh—**Piper Mountain Christmas Tree Farm** (27 Trundy Road), which offers a variety of trees—and **Nutkin Knoll Farm and Sugarworks** (269 Chapman Road), where you can find a variety of spruce trees and balsam firs. After you select your tree, drive to **Bangor's European Market** (Sunnyside Greenhouses, 177 Buck Street), where world foods, local produce, and homemade baked goods are sold. If you want to extend your day trip, skate at **Sawyer Arena** (107 13th Street, Hayford Park). The NHL-sized ice arena offers regular public skate times, but you'll need to bring your own skates.

Trip 2: Bar Harbor
Enjoy the peaceful calm of winter with a carriage ride at **Wild Iris Horse Farm**, (2 Lakewood Farm Road). Your family can choose from a private or public ride (for up to 10 people) down quiet rural roads, cuddled together under wool blankets. After your farm visit, drive to nearby **Glen Mary Park** (11 Waldron Road) where you'll find a frozen pond for outdoor skating. Bring your own ice skates.

Trip 3: Mars Hill/Presque Isle
In addition to offering downhill skiing, **Bigrock Ski Area** (27 Graves Road) in Mars Hill also has snow tubing on weekends. Kids (42 inches and taller) have so much fun sliding and spinning down the 800-foot-long hill. If the weather gets too cold, head indoors to skate at **The Forum** (84 Mechanic Street) in Presque Isle. Skate rentals, skating aids for beginners, and sleds for little ones are all available to rent.

Courtesy of Winterberry Farm, Belgrade

Index